ATTICUS

MW00623232

Cashflow & Profitability

What Law School Didn't Teach You About Running a Successful Law Firm

Mark Powers and Shawn McNalis

Cashflow & Profitability:

What Law School Didn't Teach You About Running A Successful Law Firm

Publisher: Atticus Ink
345 S. Highland St.
Mount Dora, FL 32757
www.atticusadvantage.com

ISBN: **978-0-578-75638-7**

12 11 10 09 08 5 4 3 2 1

Table of Contents

This detailed TOC is being provided to facilitate easy navigation

Chapter 4: Leverage
How To Build Profit-Centered Teams 87

Chapter 5: Expenses
What Are You Spending Your Money On? 107

Chapter 6: Speed
How the Lack of Speed Kills Your Profit Margin **129**

About the Authors

Mark Powers, president of Atticus, has been coaching attorneys on practice management and marketing for nearly 25 years. An international speaker, Mark has coached thousands of attorneys in his work with the American Bar Association, and Bar associations in Arizona, Mississippi, Massachusetts, Florida, New York, Connecticut, South Carolina, Texas and the Midwest. Mark also conducts a bootcamp-style program called the "Practice Builder" for solo, small, and mid-size firm practitioners. In addition, he leads troubleshooting retreats that deal with partnership issues, difficult retirement scenarios, client development, and productivity problems. Mark is known for his expert advice on legal marketing, and he has co-authored these books: *The Making of a Rainmaker: An Ethical Approach to Marketing for Solo and Small Firm Practitioners,* published by the Florida Bar; *Time Management for Attorneys: A Lawyer's Guide to Decreasing Stress, Eliminating Interruptions and Getting Home on Time; How Good Attorneys Become Great Rainmakers: A Breakthrough Referral Marketing Process;* and in 2013, *Hire Slow, Fire Fast: A Lawyer's Guide to Building a High Performance Team.* He has been featured in publications such as *Lawyers Weekly USA, Money Magazine, Journal of the American Bar Association, Journal of the Law Society of Scotland, Florida Bar News,* and *Massachusetts Bar Association Lawyers Journal,* among many others.

Prior to beginning work with the legal profession, Mark served as the chief executive officer and president of a multimillion-dollar, privately held company, and as a corporate manager in a Fortune 500 company based in Connecticut. A native of Massachusetts, he has a Master's degree from Northeastern University. His undergraduate studies include Bachelor's degrees in economics and criminal justice.

Shawn McNalis is a former Imagineer with the Walt Disney Company, and credits her 15-year career with Disney for her creative, collaborative approach to advising attorneys. In partnership with Mark Powers since 1995, Shawn is a senior practice advisor, director of curriculum, and trainer for Atticus. With Mark she co-authored *The Making of a Rainmaker*, commissioned and published by the Florida Bar in 1995; *Time Management for Attorneys: A Lawyer's Guide to Decreasing Stress, Eliminating Interruptions & Getting Home on Time*, published in conjunction with the ABA in 2008; *How Good Attorneys Become Great Rainmakers: A Breakthrough Referral Marketing Process* in 2009; and in 2013, *Hire Slow, Fire Fast: A Lawyer's Guide to Building a High Performance Team*.

A former columnist for *Lawyers Weekly USA*, Shawn has authored and co-authored numerous articles on law practice management that have appeared in the ABA's *Law Practice Management Magazine, Journal of the Association of Legal Administrators, ABA Family Law Section Magazine, The Florida Bar News, The Lawyer's Competitive Edge, The Florida Bar Workers Compensation Section Journal, Family Lawyer Magazine, Attorneys At Work* and *Massachusetts Bar Journal*, among many others. A faculty member of the Massachusetts Bar Association Institute in 1998 and past coach for the *Orlando Sentinel's "Career Makeover"* column, she was a contributing author for the *Association of Legal Administrators Online Encyclopedia*, published in 2002. Shawn has been a featured speaker at numerous events, including those for the Law Society of Scotland, the New York State Bar Association, the Florida Bar Association, the Massachusetts Bar Association, the South Carolina Bar, the Illinois Bar, and the Florida Justice Association.

Acknowledgements

For the many clients we work with whose dedication to the law drives them to build firms to serve their clients well, it can be a considerable challenge to also master the business aspects of their firms. Most small and mid-sized firms were begun by great attorneys with little to no business training, who have had to acquire their financial skills every day, on the job. They, like most small business owners, have been successful, while also making plenty of mistakes along the way. It's from this wealth of shared experience, combined with the wisdom of CPAs, large firm CFOs, and small firm administrators that we've drawn our ideas to create our financial best practice systems.

Thanks to Jim Fogle-Miller, retired Army Colonel and Adjunct Professor at Emory University, for patiently checking the math and making many excellent suggestions to improve both our words and our numbers. Thanks also go to Nancy Panaccione for her design talents.

We also appreciate our Atticus Partners Steve Riley, Glenn Finch and Cammie Hauser, in addition to our dedicated Practice Advisors and Adjunct Practice Advisors who coach and guide our clients every day to organize their finances and build healthy, prosperous law firms.

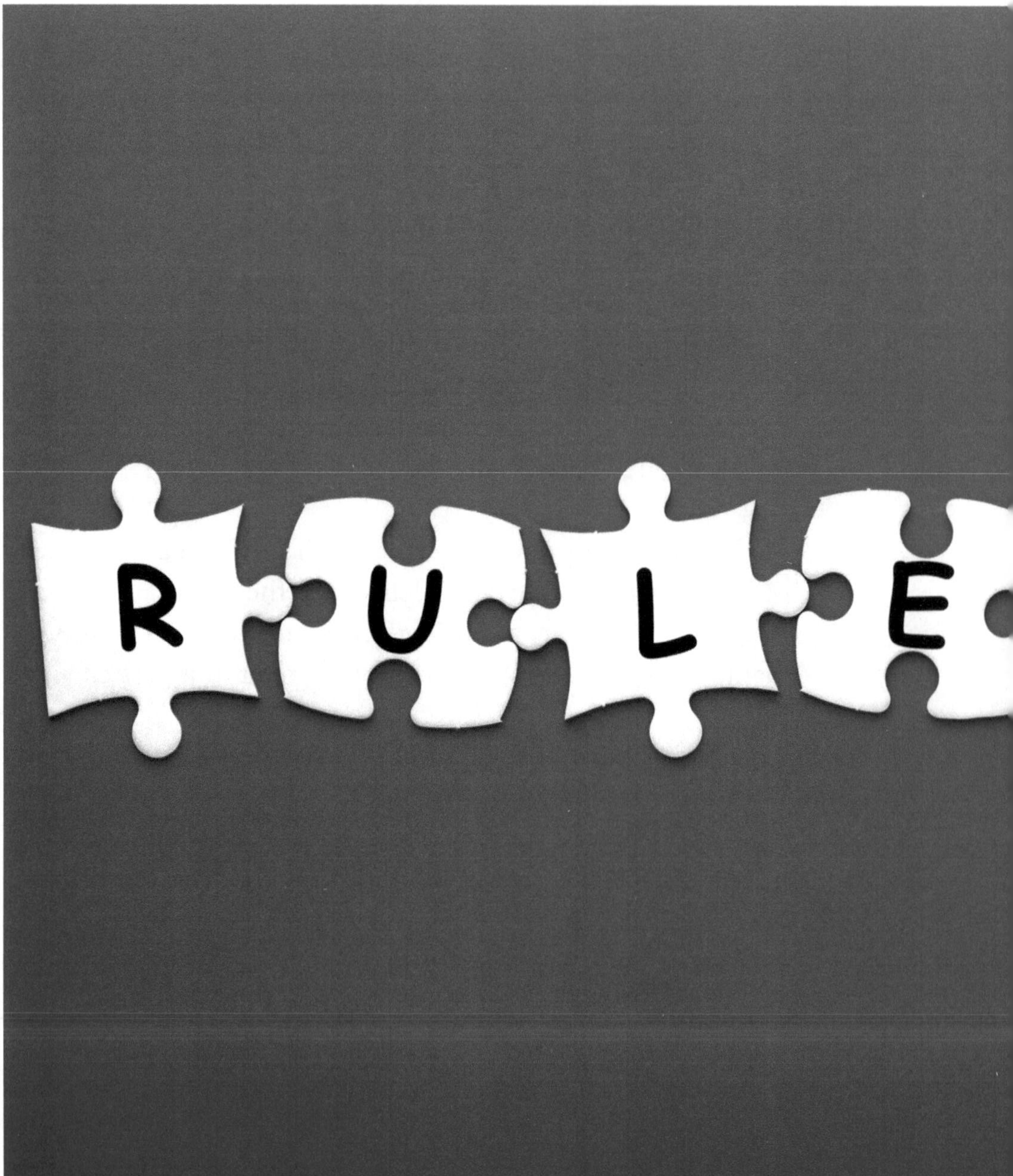
R U L E

INTRODUCTION

Maybe you're like many of the solo and small firm attorneys we work with: You have confidence in your legal skills, but you're not knowledgeable about law firm finances. Or maybe you have the financial knowledge you need, but just haven't been able to set up a system beyond what's available on your bookkeeping software. Or perhaps you've got the bookkeeping basics down and can generate a little profit, but can't figure out how to make a decent profit. A decent profit, by the way, for a service-based business, is deemed to be 25% to 30% of annual revenue – a very elusive goal for many solo and small firm practitioners.

No matter where you are in the process of building your firm's financial foundation, we've got the tools and information that can take you to the next level. There is no shame in not knowing how to handle your firm's finances. We've dealt with hundreds of attorneys who are great lawyers, but share this same problem to one degree or another. It's not your fault. The law school you attended prepared you to be a lawyer, but likely left you completely unequipped to handle the business side of practicing law. Most of them adhere to the idea that the practice of law is a lofty, mission-driven profession, aimed at serving clients and righting wrongs – a mission that should be untainted by the concerns of business. Unfortunately, many mission-driven firms don't have the opportunity to serve their clients for very long because they can't fund their mission. Don't let this happen to you.

MISSIONARY TO MERCENARY SPECTRUM

Given this gap in the legal education system, we saw the need to educate lawyers on the essential business practices they need to create a financial foundation that will allow them to prosper in their profession. On the Spectrum that spans the distance from the Missionary approach to the Mercenary one, we say there is a happy medium. And that means law firms must operate like businesses so they can *survive* to fulfill their mission.

Perhaps in the future law schools will recognize how they set up attorneys to fail by not teaching them the business skills to run a healthy practice. Until then, many attorneys will struggle and eventually go out of business because they are great lawyers, but terrible business people.

The entire theme of this book could be summed up in these words:

PROFIT IS GOOD

Unfortunately, being profitable is one of the least understood and most vilified concepts in the legal profession.

We believe profitability is what allows you to sustain and grow your firm so you can continue being of service to your clients. Our mission is to teach you what your law school education left out. In this book, we'll show you how to set up a financial foundation using our customizable templates and protocols. Building on this foundation, we'll then introduce you to a set of easy-to-follow best practices and guidelines for building a firm that's well organized and profitable. Along the way, we'll give you a road-tested bundle of tools to help you manage and maintain it.

THE RULES OF THE GAME

Here is a quick preview of the principles we'll be discussing throughout this book. Created and used by CPAs to support small business owners, almost everything we're going to explain in this book is represented by this easy-to-remember acronym: the **RULES.** Each letter represents different aspects of your firm's economic engine. The theory states that once you understand how the engine operates, you can adjust the pulleys and levers to produce the profit you want.

These guidelines are not difficult, but no one discovers them without guidance. They must be learned. Fortunately, it's not rocket science – and if you're smart enough to have earned a law degree, they will be easy for you. Here is a quick look:

R stands for **Rates and Realization,** which refers to how much you charge and how much you collect.

U stands for **Utilization,** which looks at the percentage of time in the office that is used productively by your revenue producers and timekeepers.

L stands for **Leverage,** which measures the number of producers or timekeepers per partner.

E is for **Expenses,** which addresses all the costs associated with your overhead.

S stands for **Speed,** which measures how long it takes to collect what you're owed.

We're going to explain each of these guidelines in upcoming chapters, so don't panic if these brief explanations are not enough. We just want you to have an overview of them before we go any further. But first you must create the foundation for them to rest on. To illustrate this process, we'll share a lot of real-life examples of attorneys we've helped as they build their firm's financial foundation.

Cashflow & Profitability:

What Law School Didn't Teach You About Running A Successful Law Firm

Chapter 1

BUILDING YOUR FIRM'S FINANCIAL FOUNDATION

"I f I were good at math, I would have become a doctor," joked one of the attorneys we began working with recently. This was his response to a question about how he managed his firm's finances. The attorney, we'll call him Ted, laughed a little nervously, and we suspected he was wildly disorganized in this particular area. Like so many of the attorneys with whom we work, he was a great lawyer, but his financial management skills were weak. In this case, he had flirted with financial disaster often enough to finally seek our assistance.

Fortunately, he had a part-time bookkeeper on board who was eager to help. Filled with good intentions, she was making the situation worse by flooding Ted with too much information. On a monthly basis she'd deliver a stack of reports to his office and wait to discuss them in all their glorious detail. Overwhelmed by the detail and the time it would take to digest it, he'd glance at the pile and tell himself he'd look through it when he had the time.

PROACTIVE VERSUS REACTIVE

That time never came – unless and until there was a crisis. Then, teetering on the edge of disaster, he'd give his bookkeeper the opportunity to meet with him and take last-minute corrective actions.

Like many attorneys, Ted managed his firm finances mostly by looking at his account balance. It was a highly reactive, not proactive, approach, meaning that he'd never taken the time to set up a financial foundation complete with the protocols and best practices to support it. In law school he'd learned to be a great lawyer, but he was grossly under-informed when it came to the business of running a law firm.

Similar to many small firm attorneys, he'd personally loaned the firm money to see it through the low points, and when he didn't have the money to lend, he'd taken out several line-of-credit loans to cover overhead and meet payroll. Like so many of his colleagues, operating this way left him feeling anxious and out of control.

Establish a System

To really get a grip on Ted's financial picture, we had his bookkeeper print out a Profit-and-Loss Statement for the year to-date, plus three previous years. Ideally, we like to see three to five years of historical data, especially for firms which have litigation cases that can span several years. A longer "look back," for any firm, however, allows us to see the natural fluctuations that occur in firm operations, and helps identify any seasonality inherent in the firm's business.

In addition to us helping him identify excessive expenses, calculate what his payroll costs were, and get a feel for his monthly revenues, having this information would help him construct a realistic budget for the coming year that is crucial to a firm's financial oversight (we'll expand on this in the Expenses section). We also wanted a close look at his accounts receivables to see his current realization rate. Seeing this information allowed us to diagnose many of Ted's issues and establish some baseline data.

After reviewing Ted's data, we recognized he needed help in nearly every aspect of his firm's finances. One of the biggest issues he had was a result of the firm's slow invoicing system. Central to the problem was Ted's failure to quickly and consistently review the firm's invoices so they could be sent out on time. While we set long-term goals to help him dig out of his current situation, we asked Ted to commit to monthly meetings with his bookkeeper and begin resolving his issues to get him back on track.

THE MONTHLY MEETING

Like many of our clients, he needed a systematic approach to handle his finances. If you need to do this as well, we recommend you start by institutionalizing a monthly meeting with your bookkeeper to create ongoing oversight and accountability. This meeting should be considered sacrosanct, and is designed to discuss the firm's finances. This eliminates the old habit of the bookkeeper submitting a lot of reports to the attorney and the attorney never getting around to reviewing them. This meeting enables the attorney and bookkeeper to discuss and decide how to handle billing issues, cashflow problems, unusual expenses, and productivity problems. Proactively keeping an eye on these issues and identifying how to handle or prevent them is critical to your firm's financial success.

Once this meeting is in place, you can use a couple of our basic templates to help manage and track your key financial indicators. The first one is our Financial Template. It's basically a monthly schedule to govern the firm's financial activities month in and month out. Both the managing attorney and bookkeeper follow it religiously, so each person does their part in making these activities happen consistently – and on time. More about this to come.

The second template is the Financial Dashboard – an easy to read report that summarizes and enables you to track all your critical financial indicators.

THE FINANCIAL TEMPLATE

When we met with Ted and his bookkeeper to discuss the use of a Financial Template, they immediately recognized that they did all of their financial tasks on a more ad hoc basis. We explained it's best to follow a schedule that dictates when their financial activities should happen, so they may position themselves at the most optimal times for consistent cashflow, and to ensure nothing falls through the cracks. Once it's established and followed, it prompts the bookkeeper to act, and reminds the attorneys of the part they play (especially in the invoicing and collections process), making it all happen in a timely fashion.

This was extremely helpful for Ted. When he could glance at this form and see what needed to be done on a monthly basis, it became a checklist he could use to better supervise the process and ensure that the firm's finances were being handled in a systematic, organized way. He kept a copy of this form handy to see when scheduled activities were taking place. All of the Atticus clients who use this template see it as an educational tool with a built-in structure of accountability.

This form, the Financial Template, is offered as a model, and the second is a blank template *(both found in the back of this chapter)*, which allows you to create your own version customized for your firm. If the bookkeeping software you use can perform this function, or could be modified to fulfill this purpose, all the better. If you opt to use our version, you'll find the following financial tasks featured:

1. **Prepare and send invoices**
2. **Payroll**
3. **Payroll taxes**
4. **Payroll tax deposits**
5. **Collection calls**
6. **Prep for and conduct Monthly Dashboard meetings**
7. **Pay outstanding bills**

Some additional items that occur on an annual basis and may be done by the bookkeeper or office manager include:

1. **Tax preparation**
2. **Annual budget preparation**

Once you fill out the form so it suits your needs, it can be institutionalized for use by posting it in the bookkeeper's office for quick and easy reference. We don't recommend this form be buried in a file, either paper or electronic, which keeps it out of sight. We want it on display. Many bookkeepers will make recurring appointments for these activities to show up on their calendars; this action can be very helpful. For additional reference and future training purposes, this template can be included in the firm's Policy and Procedures manual. Many firms have also used this template to help train a new bookkeeper in fulfilling their monthly tasks.

Use a Dashboard to Gain Control

In addition to the Monthly Template which prompts action on the part of the bookkeeper and relevant attorneys, another form, the Dashboard, displays the ongoing results of those actions. It's called the Dashboard because it conveniently displays the firm's key financial indicators the same way the gauges in the console of a car display speed, battery charge and fuel.

Without this basic information, driving would be a much more dangerous activity. The driver would have no idea how fast they were going, if they had enough of a charge in the battery, or whether they had enough fuel to reach their destination. Early on, the inventors of the automobile figured out how to create a Dashboard in which vital information was displayed prominently, allowing drivers to make intelligent decisions en route. Thanks to their foresight, there's no need to jump out of the car to check the amount of fuel in the tank – a simple glance at the Dashboard lets drivers know how much gas they have.

By prominently displaying your key financial indicators, our Financial Dashboard serves the same purpose. If your goal is to build a healthy, prosperous law firm, seeing your most important indicators in one place is important. Remember what a problem it was for Ted to go through a lot of detailed financial reports? Like him, you're extremely busy and many of you will not take the time to go through different reports to extract the information you need. The Dashboard brings all the important information to you at a glance, which makes it much more likely you'll read it.

We recommend that this Dashboard be prepared by your bookkeeper, who will extract the information she needs from separate reports in your bookkeeping software. If you currently have software that can assemble a report which is close to this Dashboard, we encourage you to use it. Your bookkeeper should go over everything with the attorney in a regularly-scheduled meeting. Detailed reports from the firm's bookkeeping software should be used to gather the information, and then be available to back up the summary sheet. This way the attorney can go through the attachments to find answers – if they require more information. If they do not require more detail, they can read the Dashboard, compare it to previous ones, and quickly see what financial trends may be developing.

THE ADVANTAGE OF USING A LAW FIRM DASHBOARD

Our Hourly Law Firm Dashboard (*found in the back of this chapter*), is designed for hourly-billing firms (skip to the next Contingency Dashboard for contingency firms if this doesn't apply to you), and is basically a snapshot of a firm's financial status. It gathers the most essential data from your Profit-and-Loss Statement, your hourly-billing report per attorney, your expense report, your accounts receivables report and your financial operations report.

Added to this are your monthly marketing statistics. Why should this information be included? It's vitally important to see the trends developing in this area as well. Marketing activities drive business in the door. This serves as fuel to the firm. If the number of activities start to decrease in the marketing categories, it will negatively impact the firm's cashflow down the road. Because we want you to be ever vigilant about future cashflow, we include it as a key indicator.

Here's a breakdown of each of the sections of the Dashboard. It explains which numbers are captured, and why:

1. **The Revenues Section:** Divided into two areas, the left side shows the fees and costs that were billed for the month, along with any interest billed. Listed on the right side are the fees, costs and interest payments that were collected for the month. These two sections will be out of sync with each other due to the time lag involved in collections, but will show important trends over time.

2. **The Monthly Billing Section:** (for hourly-billing practices) This section lists the total hours billed for the month by each timekeeper. A firm's timekeepers are like the engine in a car working to generate power – or in this case, revenue. When you see these numbers dropping, it means your timekeepers are not meeting their monthly goals and this does not bode well for future cashflow. Since this is the engine of your firm, it's vital to know how your attorneys are performing and how much you're collecting on what they're billing.

   If you have a flat-fee or fixed-fee practice and can attribute revenue generated by each producer, or each team, you can modify this section of the form to reflect this.

3. **The Expenses Section:** This area provides the attorney with an overview of the Fixed Expenses (those that occur monthly, such as your lease, copier and equipment rental), Variable

(those that occur periodically), and Client Reimbursed expenses, followed by the Payroll total and the Payroll taxes. All of this is totaled at the bottom, allowing the attorney to view the sum of the firm's expenditures on a monthly basis.

4. **The Accounts Receivables Section:** The top section allows the professional to see what was billed for the month against what was collected, and what was collected in the 30-, 60- and 90-days outstanding categories. Many hourly-billing firms have difficulty collecting what's owed them, and their effective hourly rate is reduced significantly due to this problem. We recommend a realization rate of 95% for hourly-billing firms, meaning that the firm collects 95% of what is owed. Seeing these numbers starkly displayed on a monthly basis keeps the focus on pursuing collections. As you'll see in the upcoming chapter on Speed, the sooner the billing is done and collected, the higher the realization rate.

   If you have a flat-fee or fixed-fee firm and are collecting all your money upfront, or half upfront and half by the final meeting, you have a lot of control over your cashflow and shouldn't have much of a collection problem. So, unless you do some work on an hourly basis or offer payment plans, you can omit this section or modify it to suit your needs.

5. **The Marketing Stats Section:** This area is dedicated to a quick summary of client development activities occurring during the month, a list of new referrals that were received, and a list of the cases being referred. As mentioned before, if the firm does not engage in marketing activities on a regular basis, future cashflow is at risk. A drop in marketing activities is an early warning sign. Many firms attach a spreadsheet containing more detailed marketing information due to the limited space available on the form, but it's important to summarize the activities in the space allotted to have an overview at a glance.

6. **The New Business Section:** This area captures the number of new client inquiry calls, the number of calls that scheduled an initial consultation, the number of engagement letters which are given to prospective clients, the number of matters closed, and how many matters are currently open. It shows the conversion of client inquiries to initial consultations, and how many clients are converted from the initial meetings. If there are a lot of qualified potential clients having initial consultations, but few people are converting to become actual clients, this is a red flag which indicates something is wrong with the consultation conversation. Take action accordingly.

7. **The Financial Operations Section:** This last section is dedicated to showing what is in the operating and trust accounts. As you know, your trust account funds are never to be used for operating expenses, which means you can't pay bills from them. Generally, trust accounts contain client retainers that can only be accessed when work is done and billed, on behalf of that client. It's not only unethical to tap into these accounts for anything other than client work that has been done, it can get a law firm in serious trouble with their local or state Bar association. Penalties for misusing this account can range from fines, to having your license suspended, to disbarment. It's one of the most common ways firms get into trouble. Think about it: If you knew that one of your colleagues was misusing funds, would you want to send him clients? Your good reputation is worth more than almost anything. Protect it at all costs.

As we've said, most of you are not trained to evaluate cashflow, and lack an adequate system to display the trends in your finances. Once completed, this easy-to-read Dashboard allows you to view the most important key indicators all in one spot. It covers areas that provide "fuel" for the firm, and allows you to identify cashflow issues before they happen, especially the following ones:

1. **Hourly billers who are not meeting their billing goals:** Address this immediately to find out if it's a lack of work, no accountability, a lack of individual billing targets, a failure to record time, or an increase in write-downs.

2. **An increase in accounts receivables:** Read the section on Realization to identify why this is happening and address the issue. There can be many issues at the root of this. The longer you wait to collect money, the less you will get.

3. **A slow-down in marketing efforts:** Get your marketing efforts back in gear as soon as possible. Unless you've just landed a huge client who will keep you afloat for a long time, failing to market predicts a future cashflow crisis.

You should review this with your bookkeeper once a month if you are in a relatively stable financial situation and cashflow is good. If, like our client Ted, you are in a financial crisis and have a large collections problem, you might need to review this form once a week.

CONTINGENCY FIRM DASHBOARD

This Dashboard *(found in the back of this chapter)*, is designed for those of you who are in contingency-fee firms, and is used monthly to provide an overview of your key financial indicators.

1. **The Revenues Section:** This part of the form lets you know how much money you've collected on a monthly basis. It's followed by a section allotted for Fee Income, and then allows you to subtract Costs Advance to calculate a Total. Alongside it, to the right, you can list how many cases were settled this month and the average value of those cases. To determine the average per case, take the Total Fee Income and divide by the number of cases. It's particularly important to track the average value of each type of case settled. Our form is highly simplified. Feel free to modify it to fit your firm and allow for every case type you deal with: motor vehicle, slip and fall, etc. Also, if you've received an extraordinary settlement,

set it aside when you calculate your average. It will artificially raise the average for all cases and lead you to draw the wrong conclusions about how your average case fees are trending. As advisors, we're always coaching our clients to continually increase their average fees (working only with better clients is one way to do it), and it's vital to track your progress.

2. **Expenses/Cashflow:** This section is designed to capture your fixed (those that occur monthly) and variable (those that occur periodically) expenses.

3. **New Business:** The incoming flow of new, potential clients this month will predict your cashflow 13 to 15 months out. You want to see the number of new intake calls keep increasing, and healthy conversion rates of qualified clients all the way up the line. There's nothing worse than spending time, money and energy on getting clients to call, only to lose them because something is off in your intake script.

4. **Marketing Stats:** Further down, in the marketing section, write down how many marketing activities you and your team have accomplished and with whom you've done them. Below that, list actual referrals by who referred them, and the type of case. These are your marketing numbers and, as we'll repeatedly say, marketing is the fuel to power your firm's finances.

By using this form on a monthly basis, even attorneys who aren't good at math can track, monitor and gain control of their finances based on the early trends revealed by the Dashboard. Most attorneys are driving blind; using a Dashboard like this puts them back in control.

A WORD ABOUT FINANCIAL PROFESSIONALS

While we will educate you about basic financial principles that are broadly used by CPAs, how you apply some of these strategies will depend on your individual situation. You live in different states, you're subject to different taxes and you operate under different business structures. Your business structure will determine how much you pay in taxes, your personal liability, and your ability to raise money. See the Business Structure Chart (*found in the back of this chapter*) to compare options. You will also be focused on different financial goals depending on your age and stage of life. We cannot address all these variables individually, and encourage you to use your own financial and tax professionals when considering any new strategy. To avoid unintended consequences, and ensure the right fit, whatever they say should supersede anything we have written.

In addition, we highly recommend hiring a bookkeeper who is referred by a trusted CPA. The CPA typically knows them and has evaluated their skills. These professionals bring a level of skill that's much higher, and they take their job more seriously than relatives pressed into service.

As we mentioned before, our client Ted had a bookkeeper (he shared her with a couple of other firms), and she was willing to help. This was a real advantage. Often, small firm owners will attempt to handle their own bookkeeping – even when their skill level is minimal. Or they'll ask their spouse, mother or aunt to handle their money because they feel they can trust them. Unfortunately, this is not always a good choice – not only because their bookkeeping skills are limited, but also because being a relative is no guarantee of trustworthiness. While the feeling of trust might be there, we've dealt with and heard many stories of wives, aunts, husbands and other relatives embezzling from their trusting relatives.

THE *FRAUD* TRIANGLE

Every couple of years we are hired by an attorney who has been the victim of fraud. As we listen to their story, it reminds us once again that crimes of fraud in most small law offices follow an eerily similar, very predictable pattern.

In many cases, the perpetrator is female – a trusted office manager or bookkeeper who has been with the firm for years and is heavily

relied upon. She may work long hours, take no time off, and have a tendency to do everything herself (which appears to be dedication but is instead a way of keeping others from discovering her questionable activities).

The victim is a typical attorney, someone who is stressed, distracted and not paying close attention to the financial side of the practice. He or she doesn't have good financial systems in place and trusts the office manager or bookkeeper to handle everything.

Financial carelessness and a trusting nature are an important part of this picture, but a couple of other ingredients must be in place before the temptation to defraud is irresistible. Cammie Hauser, CPA and Atticus Practice Advisor, says that three important elements are usually present prior to a fraud taking place. All together, these three factors are called the *Fraud Triangle*, and are well known to law enforcement officials because they tend to occur in all professional service businesses, not just law firms. Dentists, doctors, architects and lawyers tend to focus on their work and leave the administration of their finances to others. Our hope is that once these factors are clearly understood, they can be prevented from happening.

FRAUD TRIANGLE FACTORS

1. MOTIVATION

This occurs when there is a financial challenge in the life of the potential fraudster. Whether that challenge is due to a divorce, the need to pay off debt or finance a child's education, it must create significant financial pressure.

2. RATIONALIZATION/JUSTIFICATION

This takes place when the person tells herself that the attorney "won't miss a little of his money – he has too much anyway," or that the attorney "doesn't work hard enough to deserve all this money." There is clearly an underlying sense of resentment fueling theses thoughts, though it may be well disguised.

3. OPPORTUNITY

This transpires when the attorney does not have good financial oversight, lacks financial savvy, is distracted and/or unquestioningly trusts the team member who handles the money.

How can you prevent fraud from happening in your office? By making sure you don't let these three elements occur simultaneously in your firm.

This is easier said than done. In this difficult economy, many staff members are losing their homes, struggling with mounting debt, and/or giving extra financial support to grown children. There is little you can do to prevent financial pressure; it will take place.

Fortunately, most people don't give in to this kind of pressure, but it can amp up the level of temptation. Keep your eyes and ears open when it comes to the personal life of the person handling your finances. If he or she starts complaining to other team members about financial difficulties, watch them carefully. If you also notice that he or she refuses to let others help with financial tasks, works unusually long hours or doesn't take vacation time – and you have suspicions – it might be time to bring your CPA in for a surprise audit.

As for the second element of the *Fraud Triangle* – rationalization and justification – you have very little control over this silent, internal process as well. Comparing our lot in life to that of others is a natural, human compulsion, as is rationalizing bad behavior. People who work for you *will* notice the disparity between your financial status and theirs. Some will occasionally resent you for it, so your best bet is to hire someone who is bonded and insured from the start. We realize that's not always going to happen, especially in small firms where the staff wears multiple hats, so look for character flaws such as pettiness or jealousy of others, which may indicate negative tendencies.

Given the relative lack of control over the first two elements of the *Fraud Triangle*, we believe you should do everything you can to prevent the third factor – opportunity – from arising. You do this by establishing an organized, systematic approach to your finances – before someone takes advantage of you. This is one factor you have total control over, and it is your best insurance against being cheated.

The checklist on the next page, created by Cammie Hauser, allows you to rank your present cash control system to see if you are taking all precautions to protect yourself. If you answer "yes" to all 10 questions, you're in good shape. Any question to which you answer "no" indicates a hole in your system. Take the test right away and see how vulnerable you are to fraud in *your* firm.

THE CASH CONTROL SYSTEM

1. Are checks endorsed with a "for deposit only" stamp when they are received?

2. Is the person reconciling the bank statement (matching the bank balance to your balance) NOT the same person receiving (opening mail) and depositing revenue?

3. Are daily deposit totals matched to a computerized accounting total for recording revenue?

4. Are authorized signers, or those with the access to make transfers on the bank accounts, limited to partners/owners?

5. Are pre-numbered checks issued and any missing numbers investigated?

6. Are checks kept in a secure, locked area?

7. Are monthly expense items budgeted and any variances investigated promptly?

8. Are client-advanced costs reviewed by the assigned attorney monthly, if applicable?

9. Are new vendors (payments made for products/services) approved and reviewed at least quarterly by a partner?

10. Is there an independent review of cash receipts/disbursement procedures by an objective party at least annually?

THE CASE STATUS MEETING

We've talked about establishing a good financial foundation, but now we want to talk about a problem that occurs while the work is in progress. One of the most common financial failures we see is when the attorneys in a firm keep working away on files that aren't being financially supported by clients. While this will eventually show up on the Dashboard, this is something that should be recognized as soon as possible so work can be halted promptly, unless there are legitimate, extenuating circumstances (i.e., prior arrangements have been made or the case is deep in litigation).

To pre-empt this problem, we recommend that when the supervising attorney meets with their team to discuss the status of each case on a weekly or monthly basis, the financial status of the case be discussed as well. This ensures that lots of additional hours won't be spent on matters for which the firm won't be reimbursed. This is a very simple step that has a huge return for the small amount of time involved. If this is one of your firm's issues, you can improve your firm's collections immediately by adding this small step to your meetings.

At this point, we've introduced you to and discussed the most useful tools and protocols we have to help you create your firm's financial foundation. Once your monthly meeting is in place and your use of the Monthly Financial Template and Dashboard is institutionalized, you'll be able to monitor and manage your firm's finances in a healthy, proactive fashion. Now that you've done the necessary groundwork, read on to learn how to use **Rates and Realization**, the **"R"** in the **RULES,** to build a profitable firm on this foundation.

Monthly Financial Template SAMPLE

	MON	TUES	WED	THUR	FRI
WEEK 1	Collections Calls & Confirmation of Payment Plans **1**	**2**	Deposit Payments **3**	Payroll **4**	**5**
WEEK 2	Collections Calls & Confirmation of Payment Plans **8**	Monthly Invoicing Pay Bills Due 15th-31st Payroll & Payroll Taxes (Electronic Transfer) **9**	Deposit Payments & Payroll Tax Deposit **10**	Payroll / Prepare Case Dollars Inventory List **11**	Checks logged in according to payment plan agreements. Track income received, give totals. **12**
WEEK 3	Collections Calls & Confirmation of Payment Plans **15**	Reconcile Accounts Print Monthly Reports (Coordinate w/ Case Financial Status Mtg) Close previous month. **16**	Deposit Payments **17**	Payroll **18**	**19**
WEEK 4	Collections Calls & Confirmation of Payment Plans **22**	Monthly Dashboard (Cashflow Projection) Huddle w/ Attorney **23**	Deposit Payments & Payroll Tax Deposit / Pay Bills Due 1st-14th **24**	Payroll **25**	**26**
WEEK 5	Collections Calls & Confirmation of Payment Plans **29**	**30**	Deposit Payments **31**	DAILY: Computer Back-up Lock Drawers/Files Process Mail File	Help w/Phones Support Team, as needed. Also allow time for Budget/Tax Prep as needed throughout year.

Financial Template WORKSHEET

	MON	TUES	WED	TH	FRI
Week 1	☐	☐	☐	☐	☐
Week 2	☐	☐	☐	☐	☐
Week 3	☐	☐	☐	☐	☐
Week 4	☐	☐	☐	☐	☐
Week 5	☐	☐	☐	☐	☐

Hourly Law Firm Dashboard

For the Month of: _____, _____

REVENUES			
Billings for the 15th of this Month:		**Amount Collected this Month:**	
Fee Billing	$	Fee Income	$
Costs Billing	$	Costs	$
Interest Billing	$	Interest	$
TOTAL:	$	TOTAL	$

HOURS BILLED PER ATTORNEY			
	billed		(hrs.)
	billed		(hrs.)
	billed		(hrs.)
	billed		(hrs.)
	billed		(hrs.)

MARKETING STATS	
Activities:	Referral Source/Client:
Referred by:	Type of Case

EXPENSES	
Fixed Expenses	$
Variable Expenses	$
Client Reimbursed	$
Payroll	$
Payroll Taxes	$
TOTAL	$

ACCOUNTS RECEIVABLE	
Aging Summary on 1st	$
Aging Summary on 31st	$
Amount over 90 days	$
Amount over 60 days	$
Amount over 30 days	$
Amount Current	$

NEW BUSINESS	
# of Inquiry Calls	
# of Initial Consults	
# of Rep Ltr Mailed/Del	
# of New Matters	
# of Matters Closed	
Open Inven of Matters	

FINANCIAL OPERATIONS	
Operating Account Balance at month end:	$
Cash requirements for expenses next month:	$
Trust Transfer as a % of monthly billings:	$
Fixed & Variable Expenses as a % of Fee Income:	$
Income Statement Net Income Balance:	$

Contingency Dashboard

For the Month of: _____

REVENUES			
Amount Collected this Month:			
Fee Income	$	Quantity of cases settled	
Costs Advanced	$		
TOTAL:	$	Average $$ / case	

EXPENSES/CASH FLOW	
Fixed Expenses	$
Variable Expenses	$
Client Reimbursed	$
Payroll & Taxes	$
	$
TOTAL	$

MARKETING STATS	
Activities:	Referral Source/Client:
Referred by:	Type of Case

NEW BUSINESS	
# of Inquiry Calls	
# of Initial Consults	
# of Rep Letters Delivered	
# of New Matters	
# of Matters Closed	
Open Inventory of Matters	

Business Structure Chart

Business Structure	Ownership	Liability	Taxes
Sole proprietorship	One person	Unlimited personal liability	Personal tax only
Partnerships	Two or more people	Unlimited personal liability unless structured as a limited partnership	Self-employment tax (except for limited partners) Personal tax
Limited liability company (LLC)	One or more people	Owners are not personally liable	Self-employment tax Personal tax or Corporate tax
Corporation - C Corp	One or more people	Owners are not personally liable	Corporate tax
Corporation – S Corp	One or more people, but no more than 100, and all must be U.S. citizens	Owners are not personally liable	Personal tax
Corporation – B Corp	One or more people	Owners are not personally liable	Corporate tax
Corporation - Nonprofit	One or more people	Owners are not personally liable	Tax-exempt, but corporate profits can't be distributed

https://www.sba.gov/business-guide/launch-your-business/choose-business-structure

Chapter 2

RATES AND REALIZATION

How Much Do You Charge And Then Collect?

An attorney – we'll call her Susan – stood up in one of our Practice Growth programs to say that her small firm wasn't very profitable. We saw several attorneys in the group who appeared to agree that profitability in a small firm was difficult to achieve. In response to this, Cammie Hauser, a CPA who was the program facilitator, asked, "What's your typical client like?" Susan said, "Well, I work with a broad range of people." Then she added, "And I take extremely good care of my clients." From the way she said this, it was clearly important to her. Cammie nodded and said, "Of course. Now, where do you see your firm in the Missionary (mission-driven) to Mercenary (money-driven) Spectrum that we covered earlier?" Susan smiled and said, "Well, I have to admit that I'm more on the Missionary side." Dedicated and self-sacrificing, she had watched with envy as many of her colleagues appeared to be thriving. She went on to say that she had aspired to buy her own building one day, but saw that dream fading quickly.

Cammie then inquired about her rates. "I'm not the best when it comes to talking with clients about my rates. And I haven't really raised them in about 10 years." Looking around the room, Cammie said, "Thank you for your honesty. You're admitting what many people in this room are also experiencing. You're doing a lot of work for very little money." Susan nodded in agreement. Exhausted and fed up, she replied that she needed a shift in this idealistic policy. "Your low rates and generous intake policy attract a lot of clients. Unfortunately, many of them take advantage of your willingness to work even when you aren't being paid. A lot of attorneys find themselves in the same situation. It's almost a rite of passage." She continued, "Today we're going to discuss how to get out of this downward spiral. We're going to talk about the importance of properly setting up your **Rates**. It's the first **"R" in the RULES**, and it can have a huge impact on your ability to make a profit and sustain your firm."

Like Ted, the client we mentioned in the previous section, these kinds of issues are fairly common with the small and mid-sized firm owners who seek our help. When Susan stood up in this workshop, she was representing a lot of attorneys in similar situations. An excellent legal technician, motivated by her desire to serve her clients, she had set herself up to fail without realizing it. Once she learned about the **RULES**, tightened up her client selection process, raised her rates and learned to discuss them with clients, she turned her firm around.

In this chapter, we'll help you go through the same process, because almost all of you need to improve some of these elements. We'll show you how to evaluate your rates and give you various pricing strategies in case you want to shift them. We'll also give you several different methods of rolling out a rate raise. In the second part of this chapter, dedicated to realization, we'll discuss how much you collect compared to what you bill. These two issues go hand-in-hand. Throughout, we'll talk more about client selection – or the lack thereof – which was a big part of Susan's problem. It's a recurring theme for us because it is at the root of so many financial problems.

PART 1: RATES ON THE RISE

According to the Billable Hour Index in the *Clio's 2019 Legal Trends Report,* which closely follows the Consumer Price Index, hourly rates were relatively stagnant until 2014, but have been on the rise ever since. As of 2019, the average hourly rate is steady at $253 an hour. Keep in mind that the low starting rates of beginning associates are in this mix, and pulling down the overall average. If you're a partner-level attorney or the owner of your firm, your rates will be typically higher.[1]

If you haven't adjusted your rates in a couple of years, a rate raise will have an immediate impact on your bottom line and can substantially boost your profits. Susan, for example, was generating $350,000 a year in revenues. We showed her that a 5% rate raise would add $17,500 to her bottom line without changing anything else. A 10% rate raise would bump her revenues up by $35,000. This last point is important. We know how busy most attorneys tend to be. There are very few "stroke of the pen" strategies out there that can so easily add thousands of dollars to the bottom line. Let's take, for example, an attorney that is billing 1440 hours a year. This means he bills 30 hours a week for 48 weeks (two weeks off for holidays and two for vacation). We show the impact a rate raise would have on his total revenues by stepping up the rate raise in increments of $25 an hour:

At $300 an hour, he generates $432k in revenue a year

At $325 an hour, he generates $468k in revenue a year

At $350 an hour, he generates $504k in revenue a year

At $375 an hour, he generates $540k in revenue a year

The impact of these rate raises is significant. Implementing a rate raise is not only the first suggestion in the **RULES** formula; it's the easiest and quickest thing you can do to dramatically increase your profit. As we've explained to Susan and countless others, you don't have to hire new staff, retool your systems or add a practice area to make it happen. This is a relatively easy fix. To help you figure out what's right for your firm, let's discuss it a step at a time.

FIRST: DO A LITTLE RESEARCH

Our rate raise recommendations will pertain to hourly-billing, mixed-fee and fixed-fee firms (the only way for a contingency-fee firm to raise their rates is to start working with A and B clients only). The first thing you must do is research what other firms are charging for similar work in your area. Fees for legal work vary widely by geographical location. The high-powered New York law firm that charges $750 or $1000 an hour may be far above your community's price-point. So keep your research local. Talk to your colleagues about what they're charging for themselves, their associates and their paralegals, and try to understand their rationale for what they charge. If it's a coherent pricing strategy (trust us, often it's not), then their pricing strategy is probably based on some combination of the following factors:

1. **Their years of experience**

2. **Where they went to law school**

3. **What their firm has traditionally charged**

4. **What they believe their market will bear**

5. **What they believe their reputation to be**

If your colleagues are willing to discuss this subject with you, these casual conversations may reveal enough information for you to reset your pricing strategy. If competition in your area is fierce and you don't have friendly competitors who will share their pricing with you, conduct an informal survey using the "mystery shopper technique." This means you use a staff person to call around to different firms in the area, posing as a prospective client (don't use a phone with the firm name in the caller ID!), and inquire about their fees. The point of this exercise is to further understand the range of fees typical in your area for similar services. If you have a fixed-fee firm with menu-based pricing, such as an Estate Planning firm, this same exercise applies to you.

SECOND: CONSIDER WHAT DRIVES VALUE

Once you've established the range of local fees, you'll want to decide where in that range you belong. Before you finalize your thinking, examine where you land on *Cobb's Value Curve*, which starts with easily commoditized legal work and ends with firms which serve ultra-wealthy clients in high-stakes situations which require specialized knowledge.[2]

1. **Commodity:** The market for this kind of work is very price-sensitive. This will be a higher-volume, lower-price-point business model, heavily dependent on efficiency and leverage – with both people and technology. Often, the market for this kind of forms-driven work is saturated with competitors who undercut prices. Clients will buy based on price. Unfortunately, unless you find clever ways to bundle your services, the ceiling on your fees will be lower than for other firms.

2. **Brand Name:** According to *Cobb*, this client is interested in working with a trusted, well-known firm with a stellar reputation. This client typically has more complex matters which require higher levels of experience and expertise and can pay higher fees. The value for the client is in working with the firm, but is not attached to a particular attorney. There is less price-sensitivity here since the work is a step above that of commodity firms.

3. **Experiential:** This market seeks individual attorneys who possess special expertise, proprietary systems, training or experience, which makes their service more valuable than what their competitors offer. Special expertise usually translates to faster and better results for clients. This can be extremely valuable to clients of all kinds, and they are willing to pay a premium for it. These firms can offer value-based billing, as their clients are less price-sensitive and more oriented around results.

4. **Unique:** These target clients are generally high-net-worth individuals, or, if they are institutions or corporations, are facing what the author terms "nuclear events." These are high-stakes situations such as hostile takeovers, high-profile, white-collar crimes, or celebrity scandals. These clients will seek out individual attorneys who have handled similar high-profile cases. For these clients, value pricing is appropriate since winning is everything and price is no object.

Once you've located yourself on the *Value Curve,* which hinges on the type of work you do and the type of client you serve, some of you may have a few other factors to consider when setting your fees:

Are your fees subject to review by judges who won't tolerate large fee increases? This will influence what you can charge in those cases, but you may be able to raise your rates in other areas of your practice.

Do you work for institutional clients who have fixed-rate expectations? Obviously, this is an important limiting factor.

Do you occupy a Class A or B office space that's consistent with your intended rate raise? If you're in a less-than-desirable location or building and you're planning a move, you may want to upgrade your space before instituting your rate raise.

Hopefully, at this point you understand all the factors influencing your new pricing structure. If you're the sole decision-maker on this issue in your firm, you're probably getting a feel for what you should do. If this is a group decision, assemble the relevant partners to discuss these factors – but keep those with outsized egos in check as you discuss this topic. Some partner-level attorneys can be unrealistic in their views (unlike Susan, they may have exaggerated notions about their worth), and don't demonstrate good judgement on issues such as this. Keep in mind that while we encourage rate raises, we don't want you to price yourself out of the market.

THIRD: CHOOSE YOUR RATE

Now that you've done your research and looked at the full range of value drivers which should be factored in, it's time to be specific about raising your rates. This is what we typically recommend: If you're an hourly-billing firm, and you find yourself charging less than your local competitors, consider raising your rates to match theirs. Most of the attorneys we work with decide to raise their rates by 10% to 25%. If you're at the top of the market, or just not comfortable with dramatic rate raises, increase them by 5%. As we've indicated, even a small rate raise like this can make a dramatic difference.

For a fixed-fee firm, if your research revealed that your fees are lacking and you haven't raised your fees in years, consider increasing the menu price of all services by 10% to 15%. Alternatively, if your research reveals that some of your fixed-fee services are out of step with your competition, consider adjusting those prices upward and leaving the others alone.

In mixed-fee firms, where there is a fixed-fee menu of services, but additional work is billed on an hourly basis for items that fall outside the scope of work, you might consider raising just the menu items, just the hourly rate, or both. It's up to you to decide once you've done your research and surveyed your competition.

CONSIDER MOVING TO FLAT-FEE BILLING

By the way, if you're an hourly-billing firm and considering moving to a fixed-fee or value-billing approach, we encourage you to do so; it can be an extremely effective profit-building strategy if you do it right. It tends to work best for transactional practice areas that provide predictable services and don't have to deal with an adverse third party. That's why you'll find this approach commonly associated with forms-driven practices that produce wills, trusts, trademarks, copyrights, patents, contracts and agreements of all kinds.

Practice areas that must deal with an adverse third party – complex business litigation, for example – deal with much less predictability and more complications. It is possible for them to divide out and create a flat fee for some of the initial steps they take, such as sending letters or filing suit, plus a few hours of negotiation, but generally they offer a limited, well-defined scope of work they can control, with the idea of stopping and reassessing at fixed points. Some firms offer a fixed-fee-by-phase approach, with each phase price based on a specific set of assumptions. This allows the firm the flexibility to adjust for the more complex, harder-to-predict work.

Moving to fixed fees is generally best if you have a forms-driven practice and possess a lot of expertise in your field. If you and your team are well trained and extremely knowledgeable, supported by checklists, leveraged by document creation software and using scripts or questionnaires to quickly elicit the information you need from clients, you'll increase how quickly you can complete your matters. Any effort you make to systemize and streamline your processes are penalized if you charge by the hour. The efficiencies you've built into your system, which enable you to speed that case through your pipeline, will work against you. In a fixed-fee case, speed is rewarded. The less time it takes to complete something, the more profitable the case will be for you. Just be sure you can set and keep to the scope of work defined by your fee agreement. This means discussing the scope with the client and reminding them of the limits when appropriate.

Clearly, we believe that hourly-billing firms that move to fixed fees are more profitable. If you decide this shift would benefit your firm, there are many approaches to figuring out how much to charge. They generally involve adding up the fees for the hours required to do the work (including the expected number of meetings, e-mails and phone calls), and then building in a profit. You might double your fees for higher-level work.

In addition to establishing flat fees, look at the additional services typically sought by your clients, and create packages which can help shape their decision-making process and more completely address their needs. Bundling your services to create packages offers convenience, and gives you a way to explain the total scope of your offerings matched up with your clients' needs.

As mentioned in the discussion of *Cobb's Value Curve*, if you cater to a higher-end market and can offer clients special expertise, you can take more of a value-billing approach, which puts a premium on results. In this case, the actual hours are considered and added up, but they only serve as a benchmark. In this calculation, the client is interested in "paying more for results and less for effort."[3]

As a final note on the wisdom of converting from hourly billing to flat fees, most flat-fee firms are paid upfront, or collect half upfront and the rest at the final meeting. This means they have very little or no collection problems. More about this in the section on Realization.

FOURTH: How and When to Roll Out Your New Rates

Attorney Mark Metzger, Adjunct Practice Advisor with Atticus, gives this advice to those who are nervous about when to raise their rates: "When people ask me when they should raise their rates, I say there are two good times: Yesterday or today!" All kidding aside, as a working attorney, he's seen the difference a rate raise can make in his own practice, and in that of many, many others. We recommend you give yourself a little lead time before launching your new pricing structure. Since many people on your team will be affected, you may want to solicit input from some of them, or you may just need to inform them, depending on who's involved.

You'll also need to allow time for new materials or fee agreements to be printed. If your website and/or social media sites contain any pricing references, you'll want to give yourself time to adjust them as well.

Once you've allowed time to prepare, and set the date, you must consider how to make this happen as seamlessly as possible. There are several different approaches you can take. Read through the following scenarios to understand your options:

1. **New-Clients-Only Rollout:** Pick a date, usually at the beginning of a new year or new quarter, have new fee agreements and/or fixed-price menus reprinted, and raise the rates only for **new clients**. Existing clients are not impacted unless they return with new work – and then you can decide to either raise their rates or keep them where they were. This creates a little more work for the bookkeeper until all clients transition to the new rate, but it's a good way to ease into a rate raise without having to justify it to existing clients. Many of our clients opt for this approach because it is less painful – new clients aren't offended by a rate raise because they aren't attached to what your rates were in the past.

2. **Across-the-Board Rollout:** In this approach, which works best in an hourly-billing firm, a date is picked, fee agreements are reprinted to reflect the new pricing, and a letter is sent to all existing clients notifying them of the coming rate raise. Typically, the reasons given are an increase in the cost of doing business, the acquisition of a new partner, the investment in new technology, the rollout of enhanced services (i.e., a client portal), or the fact that the firm hasn't raised rates in five or 10 years (or whatever your number is) to keep pace with the cost of living. Keep in mind that no matter what your justifications are, you can expect some complaints from existing clients. The number of clients who drop off is going to be determined by how large your rate raise is – a 5% or 10% raise won't cause a huge drop-off. A 25% rate raise probably will. That might not be so bad, depending on how many C- and D-level clients you tend to attract. Also, if you send a letter, **never** make the start date retroactive. Existing clients will not appreciate the lack of advance notice, and a move like this is guaranteed to create unnecessary ill-will.

3. **Individual Rollout:** You may decide to raise rates across the board for all attorneys in the firm, by, say, 5% or 10% – or you may decide that you're only raising rates for particular timekeepers whose rates are low. Here we're referring to both attorneys and paralegals.

4. **Partner-Only Rollout:** We often recommend that partners and shareholders upgrade their rates in an effort to push work to their associates and paralegals. When doing so, they remind potential clients they work as a team, and that while they are closely overseeing all work done on the case, the associate and/or paralegal will be doing much of the work. They emphasize that this is a huge cost savings for the client. Done correctly, this has the additional benefit of shifting much of the client communication onto the associate or paralegal who acts as the partner's Designated Hitter. This means the Designated Hitters field questions as best they can, always discussing or redirecting complex questions to the supervising attorney.

5. **The A/B Rollout:** If you feel insecure about your rate raise and want to test your new fees prior to committing to a full launch, attorney Mark Metzger suggests trying this: For the next week or two (some attorneys will take a month), randomly assign all of your new intake conversations as an A or B. The A clients will hear your new pricing; the B clients will hear the old. This allows you to compare the reactions of prospective clients to your new fees. If you get instant acceptance of the new fees from at least the first three clients, declare the experiment over and commit to your new rates. If you get a lot of pushback and a low sign-up rate, experiment with a slightly lower fee.

6. **The Jerk Premium:** Some hourly-billing litigators (often divorce attorneys), raise their rates spontaneously upon hearing the name of their opposing counsel. If, during the intake conversation with a potential client, they hear they'll be work-

ing with attorneys who they know to be difficult, they'll un-apologetically raise their rates. Typically, these attorneys have experienced the drama/lack of ethics/personality issues that accompany these other attorneys and have decided they value their peace of mind more than working with this person. If the client hires them anyway, at least they'll be well paid for the additional aggravation they'll have to endure.

7. **The Upfront Retainer Raise:** For firms that have discovered they don't collect much more than what they've charged as a retainer, an increase in the upfront retainer can be beneficial. Keep in mind, though, if this applies to your firm, there are clearly some invoicing issues at play here if you aren't being paid beyond the retainer – unless that's part of the plan. If it's not, we'd venture to say you're not doing a good job of setting expectations upfront with the client about paying additional fees.

YOU WILL WORK WITH BETTER CLIENTS

Once your new pricing strategy is launched, you may lose a few prospective clients who don't want to pay your rates. Though this is natural and to be expected, we still marvel at the number of attorneys who experience barely any falloff in the number of new clients hiring them. This is especially true of prospects who come from referral sources or past clients; these prospective clients are generally less price-sensitive after they've heard a glowing endorsement from someone they know.

However, bumping up your rate will put you beyond some clients' price range, and that's okay. For Susan, this was a blessing in disguise. Slightly higher fees in hourly- and fixed-fee practices are a great way to screen out C and D clients who are often very difficult to please – and then pay slowly, pay partially or don't pay at all. If you are at all like Susan, screening out these clients will increase your profit margin all by itself, to say nothing of the effect it will have on your stress level. Instead of spending your time dealing with difficult clients, focus on A and B clients who are cooperative, who will send A- and B-level referrals, and who will appreciate you. Best of all, they tend to pay in full and on time.

While we don't recommend you grow your firm's revenues year after year by constantly raising your rates, we find many attorneys need to do it just to bring themselves up to the current local standard. Simply raising rates is just one piece of the puzzle when it comes to long-term growth strategies. Applying the rest of the strategies found in the **RULES** is what will support your growth in the long term.

As we've said throughout this section, every day we advise firms on the full range of re-engineering options for their firms, usually with the result of helping them become more productive and thus more profitable. Some want to gain efficiencies by systemizing their processes, reshaping their team, bringing on a partner, or adding new services. These are all important approaches, but most of them require major retooling, lots of disruption, and many months to implement.

Implementing a rate raise takes a little research upfront, but otherwise requires very little work to put in place. For a very low investment in time, and a few dollars to reprint materials, it delivers a very high return. The fact that it reduces the number of C and D clients you work with is an added bonus. Working with more cooperative clients who pay you not only does wonders for your stress level, it also boosts your **Realization Rate**, the second part of the **"R"** in the **RULES**, which we'll discuss next.

PART 2: REALIZATION

"What do you think your realization rate is, typically?" We were talking to a transactional attorney – we'll call him Bill – in one of our workshops. Seeing the confusion on his face, we clarified what we meant: "Your realization rate is how much you collect out of what you're owed. If you bill $100k and only collect $75k, your realization rate is 75%. You've left 25% of what you're owed on the table. Does that make sense?" Bill nodded. "Oh. You're talking about my collections. My bookkeeper would tell you that I'm not very good when it comes to collecting money."

Indeed, he wasn't. Like many small firm attorneys who bill by the hour, he was a dedicated multi-tasker who was focused on getting new clients in the door and managing his team – all while being the biggest producer on his team. In addition, he was overwhelmed by his administrative to-do list. All of this meant Bill was working late during the week and going in on weekends. When we inquired further about his collections, he said he was being paid about 80% of what he was owed. He wasn't being paid for all that extra time he was putting in. From a quality-of-life standpoint, his time would have been better spent with his family rather than donating 20% of his work product for free.

Apparently, his bookkeeper had been trying to focus him on collections for a while, urging him to call clients to ask for payment. She was extremely uncomfortable making these kinds of calls herself. Unfortunately, he was too, so the problem continued to get worse. This meant there was a hole in the firm's financial boat, and it was getting bigger.

YOU MAY NEED A BIGGER BOAT

Perhaps you're experiencing a similar situation because you're overwhelmed by everything you must do to keep your firm afloat. We see it all the time. Attorneys routinely neglect to track their collections, even though collecting money is one of the most important routes to profitability. Even if you increased your rates as we advised you to do in the last section, that alone won't ensure that your firm is profitable. If you continue to leave money on the table, your profit margin will drain away.

Worse than that, you'll also set yourself up for burnout. Working long hours and not being paid will lead you to resent your clients and question your choice of profession. We've seen it happen repeatedly. Poor realization rates can have a devastating impact on not only your firm's financial health, it can also affect your mental health as well. Unfortunately, lawyers lead all other professions in terms of depression, anxiety and alcohol abuse. As of 2018, lawyers are almost four times more prone to depression than non-lawyers, and 26% say they suffer from both anxiety and depression. Lawyers also suffer twice the normal rates of substance abuse, which is associated with higher rates of suicide among male attorneys over 50. Clearly, increased competition, elevated client expectations and the liability risks inherent in the profession are contributing to the difficulties that lawyers are experiencing.

So, it's difficult enough to be an attorney. We don't want financial stress to add to the hefty psychological burden that's already weighing down so many of you. Life is better when you're being paid for your work. When your realization rate is in the middle 90s, we know you're working with a better class of clients who appreciate your efforts and pay you in full.[4]

THERE'S HOPE

For your mental health and that of your firm, you must focus on increasing your realization rate. We find that firms which bill by the hour are usually the ones who need the most help. For them we recommend a goal of collecting at least 95% of what they're owed going forward. If your rate is lower than that, we'll provide you with lots of ideas to help get you there.

Fixed-fee firms usually need less help. They have some built-in advantages since they can often ask for full payment upfront before providing services. Because of this, they can get close to a 100% realization rate. If you have a transactional firm but you don't collect full payment upfront, consider doing so. If that's not possible, collecting full payment at or by your document delivery meeting is the next best thing.

CONTINGENCY-FEE FIRMS

Though we'll talk a lot about hourly-billing and flat-fee firms in this section, even contingency-fee firms have issues in this area. Often, the plaintiff's firms must be very persistent to get the money they're owed in a reasonable amount of time. Once a settlement is reached, the attorneys assigned to these cases tend to turn their focus to new cases instead of collecting the money they're owed on the old ones. For contingency-fee firms, we recommend you either hire a Settlement Coordinator whose bonus is based on how quickly they get the firm paid, or bonus the attorneys, in part based on how quickly the firm gets paid. It's amazing how much more quickly settlements are paid when bonuses are tied to collections. We discuss this in more depth in the chapter on Speed.

IMPROVING REALIZATION RATES

If you're an hourly-billing firm, there are many steps you can take to salvage your realization rate and keep it high in the future. Here's a quick list, after which we'll discuss each step in detail:

Hourly-Billing Firms

1. Select clients wisely, and use a Client Intake Scorecard
   (a sample can be found in the back of this chapter)

2. Clean house

3. Improve your fee discussions with clients

4. Use fee agreements, engagement letters and declination letters

5. Send more compelling invoices

6. Create a Collections Campaign with a Designated Hitter

7. Set up collection targets and timelines

Contingency-Fee Firms

1. Select clients wisely and use a two-step intake system

2. Continually clean house, using the two-step intake system

3. Monitor incoming settlements carefully

4. Incentivize attorneys by not paying bonuses until funds are received, or bonus them based on how short the wait time is until the firm is paid

CLIENT SELECTION IS THE KEY TO REALIZATION

For most firms, the first step on the road to improving your realization rate involves looking at the quality of the clients with whom you work. Like Susan in the last section – and almost every attorney we've ever worked with – many of their problems start with poor client selection.

To work with only A and B clients, you must upgrade your intake process to better screen C- and D-level clients. You've heard us say this before: Good clients tend to appreciate the work you do for them, send good referrals, behave in a cooperative manner and, in non-contingency practices, are the most likely to pay on time and in full. With these good clients your firm will be more profitable and you'll be less stressed. When clients appreciate your help and pay you for it, you're more likely to feel valued for the contribution you make, and this helps offset the heavy burden of your responsibilities. The most bitter attorneys we've dealt with are those who entered the profession driven by their desire to help others, but became disillusioned by constantly feeling they had been taken advantage of and not paid for their work. Don't let this happen to you. Focus on attracting better clients through your marketing activities, and heavily reinforce the referral sources who send good clients your way. Your collections issues will improve and so will your quality of life in your practice.

USE A CLIENT INTAKE SCORECARD

Shifting your practice to work with better clients requires you to think of each intake decision as a business decision, a decision that will either positively or negatively affect the quality of your life in your practice. Using an intake process is a good way to make sure you're only working with A and B clients.

As you read through this discussion of our system for selecting clients, look at the Client Intake Scorecard (*found in the back of this chapter*) as a reference. Listed on the scorecard are the generic qualities we deem most critical to screen for when selecting new clients and avoiding those who are problematic. We have scorecards that are very practice-specific, but, at their core, they all contain a version of the following qualities:

- **Client cooperation and credibility**

- **Ability to pay (for non-contingency practices)**

- **Case Value**

- **Type of work (is it the type of work you prefer?)**

- **Referral source**

Our ranking system of these characteristics is based on four levels of clients. We call them A, B, C and D clients. The A clients score the highest in each category; D clients score the lowest.

You can modify the form to suit your own needs. For example, some attorneys may assign a different weight to each category. Most of the hourly- and flat-fee attorneys we work with weigh the ability to pay quite heavily. For these attorneys, a client who scores as an A client in every category, but who cannot pay for services, is immediately downgraded to a D level.

For some attorneys we work with, the opposing counsel category is added and can carry a heavy weight. Their experiences with some opposing counsel have been so negative, that even if a client is a high-scorer in every category but this one, they refuse to take the case. Alternatively, some of them simply raise the cost to the client based on what they fondly call the "Jerk Premium." To them, coping with the psychological stress and extra work generated by the opposing attorney's tactics warrants the higher fee. They know what it means to enter into battle with certain attorneys and will openly discuss this with the potential client.

For an example of how a specific type of practice would customize their scorecard, here are the criteria used in one particular family law practice:

❑ **Availability of Assets**

❑ **Client Personality and Credibility**

❑ **Level of Income**

❑ **Attitude Toward Children**

❑ **Case Complexity**

❑ **Level of Spousal Animosity**

❑ **Opposing Counsel**

❑ **Referral Source**

Read through our generic version of a Client Intake Scorecard and use it as is, or modify it to suit your particular practice. Think about the clients you consider to be A level, and those who have been D-level clients. Add your own criteria to the scorecard to ensure that it reflects the issues you must consider before working with a client. In case you aren't using a systematic approach to screening your clients, we've included a chapter from our book *Time Management for Attorneys,* in our Appendix, to remind you of how the process works.

YOU MAY NEED TO CLEAN HOUSE

If you're new to the Atticus approach to client selection and you find yourself working with a lot of C and D clients who haven't paid you for the work you've done, it's probably time to clean house. To do this, you must first figure out which clients can be salvaged by paying you what they owe. Let this group of clients know you can't continue working with them until they pay their balance. If they don't comply, you can withdraw from these cases legitimately by sending a disengagement letter, except for those clients involved in litigation, which usually requires a judge's approval. For those clients you can't refer out because there's only a little left to do on their case, set a goal to finish the work you've agreed to do as rapidly as possible. And then *do no more.* If you seek payment and get paid – great! If you don't, consider it an expensive lesson. For the remaining clients, see who you can legitimately refer to other attorneys, i.e., the clients who have needs outside of your expertise, or the ones you don't get along with. Remember, in many cases, your C-level cases may be somebody else's B-level cases.

THE TWO-STEP INTAKE PROCESS

If you're a personal injury attorney, your path to a clean house is a little different. First, review and rate your inventory of cases. Then identify those low-value cases or difficult clients you shouldn't have taken on and decide how to deal with them. You might refer some out, and notify the rest that you're disengaging. Now look at the higher-value cases that may have been neglected as you and your team dealt with a bloated inventory. Focus on them and figure out how to maximize their value.

For the future, consider implementing a two-step intake process. If the facts of the case look promising upfront, and fit all the criteria on your Client Intake Scorecard *(access a sample at the end of this chapter)*, take the case for further investigation. That's Step 1. Give yourself an appropriate amount of time to determine the quality of the case. If, upon further discovery, it doesn't look like it's the kind of case you're interested in, notify the client and get the case out of your inventory. That's Step 2. By dividing up the process and giving yourself an "out" after discovery, you aren't obligated to complete low-quality cases. This keeps your average fee-per-file high and ensures you're maximizing your resources instead of clogging up your production pipeline.

TALKING ABOUT FEES WITH CLIENTS

If you're an hourly-billing or fixed-fee firm and you've mastered client selection, but you still have a problem, the breakdown, as with Susan in the previous section, may lie in your tendency to discount your fees when faced with a client in need. Though we applaud these instincts, and we encourage you to work with pro bono clients, discounting your fees for a lot of clients will work against you if you're trying to produce a profit. Remember, the mission-driven firm can only fulfill its mission if it can fund itself; a balance must be found that satisfies your drive to help others but also sustains your firm.

FEE AGREEMENTS

If you don't spend much time discussing your fee agreements with potential clients for reasons we've discussed before, you might want to reconsider that policy. They not only clarify what the firm will do and how the firm is paid – which is crucial to reducing collections – they also help to set client expectations upfront. Once you've improved your fee discussions with clients, remember to reinforce them in writing. Adding engagement letters and even declination letters, when necessary, ensures that everything is understood.

HOT TIP

Also, as we mentioned before, printing your fee schedule or fixed-fee menu of prices and then laminating it has an almost magical effect on the fee discussion. And it happens on both sides of the transaction. Attorneys report that prospective clients display a high level of acceptance when they see fees presented in this way. It allays their fear that the attorney is marking up the fees based on their perception of the client's ability to pay. And the attorneys themselves say they feel more confident when presenting their fees using this laminated form. It acts as a prop they can build a script around. This lends more authority to the conversation and makes the fees less subject to question. We know this defies logic to a certain extent, but the lamination experiment has been tried by many of our attorney clients who all give it a thumbs up. If you need to enhance your fee discussion, it only costs a couple of dollars to get a form laminated – so there isn't much of a downside to experimenting with it.

ENGAGEMENT AND DISENGAGEMENT LETTERS
(Examples of these letters can be found at the end of this chapter)

Sample Engagement Letter

When the fee agreements are agreed upon and signed, it's time to send an engagement letter. This sample letter works in tandem with the fee agreement, confirming in easier-to-understand language when the agreement was signed, who will be doing the work, what the case is about, and the scope of the services to be provided. It also reiterates the fee arrangement and states when payment is expected. It spells out what is expected of the client, and the client's contact person within the firm. It can also detail services not covered during the case if there is a need for further clarification.

Non-Engagement Letters

Of course, if you're screening clients well, there will be clients you don't want to take on because they don't fit the profile of an A or B client. If you decide you can't represent a client, you need to send a non-engagement letter. Basically, all non-engagement letters are a way to cover yourself in case you could be put in an unethical or illegal position by a potential client who either mistakenly believes or falsely claims you are representing them once you've had your initial consultation.

Non-Engagement Letter for Various Reasons

In this letter, you'll notice that the attorney says he can't represent the client for "various reasons," but, if another legal matter should arise, he hopes the client will consider his firm again. (We know that's not likely, but at least it leaves the door open.) It is your duty to tell the client that there might be time constraints on pursuing the matter, so the client should not wait to contact another attorney about the case. This letter does not express an opinion about the merits of the case because it could influence what the person will do regarding finding another attorney.

Short and to the Point Non-Engagement Letter

Short and to the point, this letter gives the reason (conflict of interest) the attorney can't represent the client, while also stressing that the declination expresses no opinion about the merits of the case. Time limits are addressed, and the attorney "strongly" recommends the person consult another lawyer about the matter.

Non-Engagement Letter after Research

This letter tells the client the firm will not represent him in his case because they found there is no enforceable legal basis for doing so. This opinion is based on case law, with examples cited. The client is urged to contact another attorney for a second opinion because time limits may apply. Documents are returned. In cases such as these, you're protecting the client and yourself by being prompt with your letter declining to take the case, advising him to seek another opinion, and reminding him of the time constraints in doing so.

Disengagement Letter for Unpaid Fees

Use this letter when a client owes you for services you have performed but refuses to pay – even though they signed the fee agreement. This informs the client that the firm will file a motion to withdraw as counsel unless the bill is paid by a certain date. The client is informed that he'll need to find other representation because of specific (if known) time constraints. If the fees are left unpaid, the client is told the law firm will return the files or forward them to a new attorney, but, after a certain number of years, the files will be destroyed.

INVOICING BEST PRACTICES

It's important, if you're a firm that must send monthly invoices, to go about it in the right way. Remember the Monthly Financial Template we introduced you to in the first section? It sets up the ideal timeline for the entire invoicing process and should be followed to ensure that your invoices are created, reviewed and sent out on time every month.

Our client Bill was managing his firm's billing process in a very ad hoc fashion. This meant his cashflow was unpredictable as well, adding to his feelings of not being in control of his firm. As you'll learn in the section on Speed, long time lapses between the time work is done and recorded, then entered into the billing system and then sent out, degrades the amount that is ultimately collected. More about this later.

For now, just know that approaching your invoicing in a systematic and timely manner is very important to preventing low realization rates in the future. Once your routine is reliably in place, your next task is to prepare your invoices in a way that motivates clients to pay. All too often, attorneys or their staff rush to get their invoices completed, and shortchange the recipient by not adding enough detail to explain the work that was done. The firms that do attempt to add detail will often load up their invoices with abbreviations that are difficult to understand and add to the client's confusion. This is not a successful strategy if your intent is to have your invoices paid without a lot of questions and misunderstandings.

Studies show that action words such as *"conferred with," "researched," "filed"* and *"prepared"* provide a little more of a narrative quality to your invoices, and more convincingly communicate to the client the nature of the work that was done. It's easy for the client to visualize a conference occurring or research taking place – these are not obscure terms and they help to paint a picture of the activities the attorney's office undertook on the client's behalf. Anything that helps to explain the invoiced activities is going to result in an invoice that is more readily paid. This is especially important for attorneys who work with clients unaccustomed to using legal services. These clients feel they are at an extreme disadvantage when it comes to dealing with attorneys, and are very sensitive to overpaying. Invoices that arrive with a great deal of blank space leave already skeptical clients to wonder what has really been done to warrant the attorney's fees. Don't do this to your clients. They should be supplied with a lot of information so they never question what has been done on their behalf. Your invoices are more likely to be paid if you include detailed descriptions.

In addition, any wording that speaks to furthering the client's goals is seen as positive by clients, as is the use of personal notes scribbled on the invoice. Some attorneys will note time for phone calls and will write "no charge" on them if the call was short. This can soften the impact of a hefty invoice. In select situations, discounts can also be offered as an incentive to pay in full by an early date. Statements such as "10% discount if paid in full by _____" can encourage some clients to pay early. We advised Bill to gather his team together and do a lunchtime seminar on how to properly prepare their invoices going forward.

Once the invoices are sent, make sure they are monitored closely and calls are being made to the clients at the five- or 10-day past-due date. This will go a very long way to speed up payments and prevent collection issues. These are not difficult calls to make – they should be done with a friendly, client-service-oriented tone. Your bookkeeper can say something like, "We were concerned when we didn't receive your payment. Would you like to put this on your credit card?"

If this is done, the attorney's collection problems will be reduced because they have taken two important steps: Devised their invoices so they are more likely paid, and they've followed up within five or 10 days on potential payments instead of waiting weeks and months to discover there was a problem.

What's Outstanding?

Now that we've discussed ways of improving your system for the future, let's get back to assessing and then collecting what is owed to you from the past. If you have a bookkeeper, or use accounting software, you should be able to pull a report that tells you what's outstanding in the 30, 60, 90 and 120+ days past-due categories. This is important.

When we first begin working with a firm, we help them assess what is outstanding (that can be a wake-up call), and then we give them strategies to collect it. Unfortunately for Bill, there were $40k in outstanding receivables that were not going to come in on their own. We helped him mount a campaign to collect it.

THE DESIGNATED COLLECTOR

We typically ask the attorney to elect someone in their office to be what we call the Designated Collector. Many bookkeepers are introverted by nature and shrink from the prospect of making difficult calls like these. Who else could it be? An associate, an office manager, even a paralegal – if they fit the needed qualifications.

THE RIGHT PERSONALITY

It's going to be this person's responsibility to make collection calls on a consistent basis and track the revenue generated by all of their efforts. So, it's important to use someone who possesses the following characteristics:

1. Capable of being friendly but firm

2. Can be respectful and service-oriented on phone calls

3. Persistent and patient enough to make repeated contacts in the form of more phone calls, letters or e-mails

4. Detail-oriented enough to document the status of every client in every phase of the process

5. Capable of creating a spreadsheet to track progress, or able to use reports available in their bookkeeping software

6. Motivated enough to do this work and unafraid to negotiate with difficult clients

If the Designated Collector is financially motivated, it helps to create a bonus program for them. This technique is especially useful if the collection process will add substantially to their existing workload. Bonuses are usually based on how much they collect by agreed-upon deadlines. Bill ended up using an older paralegal in his office. Since non-attorneys can't split fees with attorneys, he couldn't give her a percentage of what she brought in. Instead, he gave her a choice of a cash bonus in an agreed-upon amount (based on the completion of the project and not a percentage of what she brought in), non-monetary rewards such as gift certificates, or time off.

THE COLLECTIONS CAMPAIGN

Before you begin your collections project, you should first check any state-specific guidelines that apply to debt collection calls or contacting those who owe you money. Depending on the amount of receivables the Designated Collector is working on, they may need to launch a collection call campaign in which calls are made every day for one or two hours. This could go on for a period of three to six months until all the collections are caught up. There will be many missed calls and phone messages left behind as many clients will be difficult to contact. Persistence is key here. It is all too easy to give up when contact is not readily made, but it is worth persisting to collect as much money as is possible.

Before any calls are made, the Designated Collector should confer with you or the responsible attorneys about all the clients on the accounts receivables list. These debts must be discussed on a case-by-case basis. The oldest accounts receivables should always be the highest priority, with those in the 60 and 30 days past-due categories as the next priority.

We prepared Bill for the fact that it may be necessary for him to participate in collecting certain debts, as his personal intervention would likely bring the best results. This might mean he has to pick up the phone and call certain people, or even pay them a visit. Every debt and debtor is different, and once you have your list you can divide them into two categories: negotiable and non-negotiable. First, let's look at the negotiable debts as they're the easier category to deal with:

NEGOTIABLE SITUATIONS

The client wants to pay but is temporarily unable to do so:

Work with the client to pay by credit card, create a payment plan, barter for a service or something non-monetary. Examples we've seen include signed sports memorabilia, catering for a firm event, cleaning services, jewelry, artwork and rare books. This is not something you want to do very often for obvious reasons, but something is better than nothing.

The client can pay, but is stalling:

Find out why they're stalling and then offer the same options previously mentioned.

The client is in a dispute with the firm:

If the dispute is minor and the person is reasonable, the Designated Collector may be able to resolve it and collect payment. If not, they may have to involve the attorney and/or offer a discounted fee, depending on the situation.

Those are the options for the easier situations. If clients still resist payment after you've made reasonable accommodations and you're sure that pursuing them further won't push them to file a grievance or post negative reviews online, you can take tougher measures. Usually that means sending a final demand letter by certified mail, return receipt requested, which states the client has five, seven or 10 days to pay in full. It may further notify the client that if payment is not received, the file will be turned over to a collections firm. Before sending a notice like this, be sure to check local and state rules to ensure you're in compliance.

NON-NEGOTIABLE SITUATIONS

Now let's look at the options you have when dealing with more problematic clients and their situations:

The client is truly destitute:

Most likely you'll have to forgive or write off this debt. In some cases, you may be able to barter for a service or something non-monetary.

The client is upset and will file a grievance if the debt is pursued:

Tread carefully here. Even if you are justifiably owed the money, the payment is usually not worth the time and embarrassment involved in going through a lengthy grievance process. We've coached many a client through this process and they would tell you it's never worth it.

The client is upset and threatens to leave scathing, online reviews about you:

Tread carefully here as well. Sometimes this happens by itself; sometimes this is combined with filing a grievance. Though you don't want to be held hostage by these kinds of threats, this is serious. Your ability to get negative reviews removed is extremely limited. The best you can do is to dilute them with a flood of positive reviews – and that will take work. Sometimes it's just not worth it to pursue payment if you must deal with someone this vindictive.

It is important to rank debtors into these negotiable and non-negotiable categories, as not every situation is the same. Only those folks in the negotiable category should be seriously pursued for collections. The negotiating options outlined should be predetermined for each client, and the Designated Collector should understand what their options are before they communicate with the client.

The overall tone of the collection call, e-mail, letter or text, especially the initial ones, should be very client-service oriented, yet very straightforward. The assumption at the beginning of the process is that the client will cooperate with the firm and wants to resolve the situation.

Since we know that's not always the case, the Designated Collector should document everything, assemble the results in a weekly report for the attorney, calendar the next follow-up action, and send confirmation notes to the client after each contact to reinforce what was negotiated.

COLLECTION CALLS: ARGUMENTS AND RESPONSES

To help with difficult calls, our Collection Calls Arguments/ Responses form *(found in the back of this chapter),* supplies you with sample responses to use when clients question the amount of their debt, become uncooperative, or voice resistance. The Designated Collector can study these scripts in advance and be prepared for what the debtors may say to them. Difficult clients can be very creative when they do not want to pay.

Collecting money that is due can be a challenging task, but, by using a Designated Collector, even money that has been outstanding for many months can be collected. It's not a waste of time and can produce more revenue in a shorter amount of time than your best marketing efforts.

CONSIDER CREDIT CARDS

Another way to ensure you're paid is to offer your clients the credit card option. Besides the ease of payment, having a credit card on file establishes a client's creditworthiness and your ability to get paid on time. Using plastic places the burden for collections on the credit card company instead of your office. Plus, if the credit card is refused when it is submitted, the attorney immediately knows that this person has credit problems and may be a financial risk. For a more in-depth discussion of credit card use, skip to the chapter on Speed where we examine this topic in detail.

RETAINERS

Collecting a retainer is a great way to ensure the client is as invested in your services as you are. A retainer is, at its most basic level, money the client pays upfront to secure your expert legal services; it is a down-payment on the representation you'll provide. If a client pays you on the front end, she's more likely to be motivated to sign papers, provide documents and respond to your requests in a timely fashion. Some firms ask for upfront retainers and then bill the client on an hourly basis going forward. Firms that handle large cases often set up an Evergreen Retainer, which requires that a certain level of funds be kept on account, to be replenished regularly. Be sure to monitor this and send a Replenishment Letter *(see sample at the end of this chapter)* to remind the client of their obligation when the funds drop below the agreed-upon level.

IN CONCLUSION

In this chapter we've talked about client selection, working with only A and B clients, cleaning house, improving fee discussions, using fee agreements, using engagement and disengagement letters, sending more compelling invoices, appointing Designated Collectors, conducting collection campaigns, allowing payment by credit card, and collecting retainers. Every one of these options plays a role in your firm realizing as much money as possible.

In the next chapter, we'll talk about utilization, which is the percentage of time a team member works in your firm that is either revenue-producing or billable. Understanding and improving this metric is one more step on the way to increasing profits, so let's dive in.

ENDNOTES

1

Clio's 2019 Legal Trends Report,
www.clio.com/legal-trends/2019-report

2

William C. Cobb of Cobb Consulting,
www.cobb-consulting.com

3

William C. Cobb of Cobb Consulting,
www.cobb-consulting.com

4

Another Lawyer Suicide: How the Psychology of
Being a Big Firm Lawyer Can Tear You Down,
2018 www.bcgsearch.com/article/90049718

CLIENT INTAKE SCORECARD

	Client Personality	Type of Case	Case Value	Collectible	Referral Source	Client Expectations
A	Low Maintenance & Cooperative	Preferred Work (enjoy the work and it's within your practice expertise)	High Fees	High (pays retainers/bills promptly & doesn't question invoices/ statements)	Very Good	Realistic Expectations
B	Low Maintenance & Cooperative	Semi-Preferred Work	Medium Fees	Medium	Good	Realistic Expectations
C	High Maintenance & Not Cooperative	Non-Preferred Work	Low Fees	Low or Slow Pay	Yellow Pages (or referred by a C client)	Unrealistic Expectations
D	High Maintenance Very Difficult	Work Out of Your Practice Expertise	Low Fees or No Fees	Very Low or No Pay	Yellow Pages (or referred by a D client)	Unreasonable Expectations

NOTES: _____

(Note: if a client scores low in the "Collectible" column, it drops their score across the board. If your firm can't collect, it does not matter how well the person scores in other categories)

SAMPLE ENGAGEMENT LETTER

DATE

NAME
ADDRESS
CITY, STATE & ZIP

Re: [Subject]

Dear:

Based on our conversation of [*date*], the purpose of this letter is to confirm that [*insert firm name*] will represent you in [*describe matter*]. We will provide the following services: {*list services to be provided*].

Attached for your use is information on our billing and reporting procedures. Our fee is [*insert dollars per hour*] for services performed by lawyers of this firm and [*insert dollars per hour*] for services performed by our non-lawyer staff. You will also be billed for expenses incurred on your behalf.

Our expectations of you are: [*list any expectations concerning payment of bills, responses to requests for information, etc.*]

Your primary contact for this matter will be [*insert lawyer's name*]. If you have any questions about your case, you should contact him/her directly.

This firm has not been engaged to provide the following services: *[list services].*

Sincerely Yours,

Reference: LOMAS, The Florida Bar

NON-ENGAGEMENT LETTER FOR VARIOUS REASONS

NAME
ADDRESS
CITY, STATE & ZIP

RE: [SUBJECT]

Dear:

You have contacted this firm and requested that I evaluate whether the firm will represent you in a claim you believe should be filed against [*insert appropriate name(s)*]. I met with you yesterday and have reviewed various documents you left with me. I enclose those documents for your file.

I appreciate the confidence you have expressed in our firm, but, for various reasons, the firm has decided not to represent you in this matter. However, if you have a need in the future for legal assistance, I hope you will again consider our firm.

You should be aware that the passage of time may bar you from pursuing whatever, if any, claim you may have against [*insert appropriate name(s)*]. Because time is always important, and could be critically short in your case, I recommend you immediately contact another firm for assistance.

In declining to undertake this matter, the firm is not expressing an opinion on whether you will prevail if a complaint is filed. You should not refrain from seeking legal assistance from another firm because of any interpretation you may place on this firm's decision not to go forward with this matter.

In accordance with our standard policy, we are not charging you for any legal fees or expenses. While we do charge for evaluating cases, that is only when we express an opinion on the merits of the case to the client. Since we are not expressing an opinion in this instance, no charge is being made.

Although I believe this letter fully covers all pertinent matters, please call me if you have any questions.

Very truly yours,

Enclosures

Reference: LOMAS, The Florida Bar

SHORT AND TO THE POINT NON-ENGAGEMENT LETTER

(May be sent by certified mail, with a return receipt requested)

DATE

NAME
ADDRESS
CITY, STATE & ZIP

RE: [SUBJECT]

Dear:

The purpose of this letter is to confirm, based on our conversation of [*date*], that [*insert firm name*] has decided to decline this case because [*insert reason for declination, if possible and appropriately state it*]. Our decision to decline this case should not be construed as a statement of the merits of your case.

You should be aware that any action in this matter must be filed within the applicable statute of limitations. I strongly recommend that you consult with another lawyer concerning your rights in this matter.

Very truly yours,

Reference: LOMAS, The Florida Bar

NON-ENGAGEMENT LETTER AFTER RESEARCH

NAME
ADDRESS
CITY, STATE & ZIP

RE: [SUBJECT]

Dear:

Pursuant to my letter of [*date*], we have conducted [*legal research or investigation*] to determine whether or not we felt you had a claim that could be asserted against [*insert appropriate name(s)*].

The result of our [*research/investigation*] indicates that there is not enforceable legal basis for maintaining an action against [*insert appropriate name(s)*].

(optional paragraph)

Our opinion is based upon our preliminary research; however, we have found [*insert number of cases)*] cases that support our conclusion.

We urge you to consult another lawyer if you wish a second opinion. Time limitations may affect your rights to pursue a claim; therefore, you should act promptly in consulting another lawyer, or otherwise pursuing your claim.

At this time, however, we are unable to proceed on your behalf. We are returning your original documents to you.

Thank you for your interest in our firm.

Very truly yours,

Enclosures

> **If you decide to decline representation after research or investigation, you should protect yourself and your client by: (1) promptly advising the client in writing of your decision not to take the case or matter; (2) be certain to inform the client of his or her right to contact another lawyer for a second opinion; and (3) inform the client that his or her prompt attention is required. Disengagement and nonengagement letters are especially critical when a lawyer decides not to continue past a specific stage in the case.*

Reference: LOMAS, The Florida Bar

DISENGAGEMENT LETTER FOR UNPAID FEES

Dear Mr./Mrs._____:

When I undertook to represent you concerning [describe nature of representation, including case number, if any], you signed a fee agreement agreeing to pay for the legal services provided to you and the costs and disbursements made on your behalf. At the present time, our records reflect that you have not paid our invoices in a timely manner as you agreed you would.

Our records reflect that you have paid [report amount], leaving a balance of [report amount], which is now due and owing. Due to the apparent breakdown in our professional relationship, enclosed please find a Motion to Withdraw as Counsel, which I intend to file. I will be happy to continue to represent you if we can make acceptable financial arrangements in the very near future. Otherwise, my further representation of you has terminated.

If you wish to be represented in this matter, you should contact another attorney immediately. Keep in mind that, if your case is not filed in a timely manner, you may be barred forever from pursuing your claim. [Include specific time limit, if known]. You may wish to call the Lawyer Referral Service at [provide number].

Please contact our office to make arrangements for the return of your file. I will be happy to give it directly to you or to forward it to your new attorney, if you wish. It is our policy to maintain a file such as yours for [insert number] years, after which time it will be destroyed. I look forward to hearing form you soon regarding these arrangements.

Very truly yours,

Reference: Ohio State Bar

COLLECTION CALLS ARGUMENTS/RESPONSES

When Clients Won't Pay: How Firms Must Respond

Argument: Your firm's rates are too high or you charged us too much.

Response: I'm sorry you weren't happy with the pricing. On what basis do you feel our rates were inappropriate?

Argument: The attorney quoted X and the bill says Y (much higher).

Response: Let me walk you through what was supposed to be done for X. After we commenced the matter, it was more involved than anyone anticipated. Did you ask the attorney to look at additional aspects of the matter?

Argument: I haven't paid because I sent a letter to the attorney.

Response: If you will share with me the issues to be addressed, I will discuss them with your attorney and get back to you.

Argument: I sent a note with a partial payment and I've not heard back.

Response: Please send me a copy of your letter and cancelled check. I will give it immediate attention and get back to you.

Argument: The charges were not in accordance with the policy we have with your firm. We don't pay for X.

Response: Do you have an engagement letter documenting which services are to be charged?

Argument: I don't like the work that was done. The attorney spent too much time on certain things and did work that was not authorized.

Response: If you can provide some specifics, I'll be happy to pass your comments on to the attorney.

Argument: I didn't know that charge was outstanding. Since I haven't received a statement for a year, I thought you wrote off the balance.

Response: Statement and reminder letters are mailed at the attorney's direction. This came to light as we were reviewing all of our outstanding receivables.

Argument: I never got that bill.

Response: I'm sorry. Give me your e-mail address and I will get a copy of it to you today.

Argument: That's all been paid. You haven't properly applied it to our account.

Response: We have no record of receiving payment. Please send a copy of the cancelled check; we'll investigate and get back to you.

Argument: Our cashflow is tight. We have a deal closing in a few weeks after which we can make payments.

Response: Can you make partial payments in the interim? When do you expect your cashflow to improve?

Argument: The deal didn't come to fruition, so we're not paying you.

Response: Please check your engagement letter. Did we agree to bill the work on an hourly basis or by result?

Argument: Because of cashflow problems, the attorney told us to pay when we can.

Response: Although the attorney has offered some partial assistance, you still need to make partial payments to reduce the balance. We expect you to increase payments as your company's financial position improves.

Argument: Your attorney botched up the deal and cost me thousands of dollars. You're lucky I haven't sued.

Response: Explain what you are unhappy about and I will discuss it with the responsible attorney and get back with you.

(Source: CMS Consulting Group, Inc.)

REPLENISHMENT LETTER

Re: (Matter)

Dear Client:

This letter is sent to you as a reminder regarding your trust account deposit with this firm.

As you know, when we mutually agreed to establish an attorney-client relationship in connection with the above-referenced matter, you signed a written representation agreement. That agreement requires a deposit be maintained at all times. Unfortunately, it appears that your trust account deposit has fallen below the required level. After our most recent billing, $_____ remains outstanding in unpaid fees and costs, and $_____ is required to replenish your trust account deposit.

Please send this firm a check in the amount of $_____ for the outstanding billing and deposit replenishment no later than _____, 202_, at 5:00 p.m. If we do not receive the full amount before that time, or make other mutually acceptable written arrangements, this firm must consider terminating its relationship with you and withdrawing from representing you in the above-referenced matter. This firm and I want to continue to represent you. However, we must insist that you adhere to the terms of the representation agreement.

If you have any questions or need further information, please do not hesitate to contact me. I look forward to receiving the above amount and continuing our professional relationship. Thank you.

Very truly yours,

[Attorney/Administrator]

Chapter 3

UTILIZATION

How Productive Is Your Team?

"How many hours are your associates typically in the office, Chris?" We were addressing the question to an attorney in our Practice Growth Program who had an hourly-billing practice. There were about 30 other attorneys in the room from firms of all kinds. "We want the rest of you to jot down a number as well. List each associate and then write down how long they're typically in the office. Is it eight hours a day? Or is it 10? Make a list of your paralegals as well, and jot down their names and what's typical for them. Be sure to note the hours of your part-time people as well." Some participants groaned, saying they didn't know the exact number. We asked them to estimate what they generally thought it was for each person.

A contingency-fee lawyer raised his hand and said, "I don't bill by the hour. Do I have to do this exercise?" An Estate Planner who charged on a fixed-fee basis asked the same question. We nodded and explained that the **"U"** in the **RULES** stands for **Utilization**. "Utilization looks at what percent of a typical workday is devoted to production. No matter what kind of practice you have, this concept applies across the board. It just gets measured differently. Those that bill by the hour use their team's billable hours to track this ratio. Contingency- and flat-fee firms generally look at revenue production to measure utilization."

"Now, next to each name, list how many billable hours that person charges a day if you're in an hourly practice. For the rest of you, list the productive or revenue-producing hours you think your team members spend out of the entire time they're in the office. The number will be different for each person. We're trying to determine the percentage of time your producers are in the office working on billable and revenue-producing tasks compared to just being present."

We called on Chris again to see what his numbers were. He had two associates and three paralegals. One of his associates, for example, put in 10-hour days consistently. Typically, though, the associate billed only five of those hours. "That's a 50% utilization rate, which, by today's standards, is pretty good." Surprised, Chris said, "But he looks busy ALL the time." We nodded. "Absolutely. But is he busy doing the right things? Or have you loaded him up with a lot of administrative duties and other non-billable projects? Your job as a business owner is to maximize each revenue producer's ability to generate revenue. If someone is working at 50% capacity, you're paying for a lot of time that isn't being used productively."

As bad as it sounds, if Chris's associate was actually being productive for 50% of his day, he was beating the national average by almost 20%.

THE STATISTICS ARE GRIM

Based on the recent findings of *Clio's 2019 Legal Trends Report*, modern-day law firms have shockingly low utilization rates. On average, lawyers who work an eight-hour day are only productive 31% of the time. This translates to an astonishingly low 2.5 hours of productive time that's captured, and, due to write-downs, only 81% of that is actually billed. Add in the average collections rate of 86% and the value corrodes even further. According to this current survey, here's how it unfolds:

1. **Lawyers work an eight-hour day.**

2. Out of these eight hours, only 2.5 hours are recorded as billable.

3. Of the 2.5 hours that are captured, only 1.7 hours are collected.

The value corrosion that occurs throughout this process and the financial impact of this scenario is devastating.

HERE'S WHAT HAPPENS:

1. Lawyers who bill out at the average industry rate of $253 an hour could expect to generate $2,024 if they billed for an entire eight-hour day.

2. But, at a 31% utilization rate, their daily earning potential shrinks to $627.

3. When the realization/collections rate is factored in, their effective daily earnings drop to $437 a day.

4. This survey tells us that the daily earning potential of today's attorney is less than 22% of what it should be if they were working at full potential.[1]

ADDING IT UP

Let's play this out a little further to see what the financial impact would be over the course of a year – in a slightly more perfect world. Here we'll assume our model lawyer is billing six hours a day (not an unreasonable expectation), and the firm's collections are at 90%. What kind of annual earning potential would they have under these conditions?

1. If the lawyer were working at 75% capacity, billing the industry average of $253 an hour, the daily earnings would be $1,518.

2. That $1,518 multiplied by five days would generate $7,590 a week.

3. $7,590 a week multiplied by 48 weeks a year (this assumes time off for vacation and holidays), means the annual revenue generated would be $364,320. Let's reduce that by the 90% collections rate for a total of **$327,888**.

Now let's compare this more perfect year of production with the modern-day reality that includes a 31% utilization rate paired with the low national average realization/collection rate of 86%:

1. At a 31% utilization rate, billing at $253 an hour and factoring in Clio's reported industry average realization/collection rate, this attorney generates $543.95 a day.

2. $543.95 a day multiplied by five days is $2,715.75 a week. (At a 31% utilization rate, it takes this attorney substantially longer to generate what our full capacity attorney generated in several days.)

3. If we multiply $2,715.75 a week by 48 weeks a year (still giving time off for vacation and holidays), the associate has generated **$130,548** per year.

Compare the **$327,888** in revenues generated by the attorney working at 75% to the **$105,840** generated by the attorney working at 31%. It's the same eight-hour day, but what a dramatic difference between the two outcomes. To keep it simple, we haven't even factored in the salary and overhead costs associated with these producers. We'll cover that in a moment. Right now, we're just looking at how the revenue triples when producers work at a higher – but still reasonable – level of capacity.

We're not advocating that you become slave-drivers focused only on revenues and nothing else. But most of you could improve the utilization rates of your producers to a reasonable level and immediately increase the revenue they produce. Think about it: You're not asking them to spend additional time in the office; you're just asking them to be more efficient with the time they're there. Working smarter, not harder, is more than a cliché; it's the core concept in this approach. We're not asking you to recruit, hire and train new associates to realize increased revenues. You just have to maximize the utilization of your existing team members. And then watch as this increase is multiplied by every person on your team – because, trust us, no one is getting anywhere close to 100% utilization.

This is also true for those of you who have flat-fee or contingency-fee firms – your team members suffer from all the same issues that impair productivity. To understand how to measure utilization in your firms, skip ahead to the section entitled *What's the Rule of Three?*

For the rest of you, let's get back to Chris in our program. When we said he could dramatically increase the revenue production of his associates, he looked doubtful. Surrounded by fellow skeptics, other hands shot up with questions. "You can't expect an associate to bill all of their time in the office. That's not realistic." We agreed. "That's why we did the math based on a 75% utilization rate. However, for many of you, just getting your team members up to 50% would be a huge improvement." Others chimed in. "Our people are already stressed. We can't ask them to do any more. It's unrealistic." Lots of heads nodded in agreement. We explained that our goal was to get their teams to work smarter, not harder. "Don't mistake busy-ness for productivity. You may think they're being productive; in fact, they might think they're being productive – but it's not always the case."

In some work settings, utilization – or the lack of it – is easier to spot. If you were building widgets in a factory using an assembly line that constantly broke down, allowing you to use it only 50% of the time, you'd see the problem immediately and have it fixed. Or, if your assembly line worked but your workers spent all their time in the back, searching for parts, one glance at the factory floor would reveal that there's a problem. But low utilization rates are not so visible in the legal workplace.

Your firm is no doubt bustling with activity and team members who appear to be busy, so it's easy to think that everyone is being productive. But the truth of the matter is, appearances can be deceiving. And, since many small firm teams become like families who don't hold each other closely accountable, if management isn't tracking this issue, there are often no consequences. Instead, the team's production quietly declines as management wonders why everyone is so busy – but they're not making much money.

So, if you're wondering why you're not profitable, look closely at the utilization rate of your team members. It's one of the most important management metrics that you've never heard of, and is considered one of the most powerful profitability levers because it reveals huge amounts of excess production capacity that's being wasted, or, at best, misdirected.

WHAT'S THE *RULE OF THREE*?

A very simple calculation to determine if revenue-producers are fulfilling the basic financial requirements of their position is called the *Rule of Three*. This general rule of thumb states that by generating three times a producer's salary, an individual is meeting their responsibility to the firm to cover their salary, their overhead and their contribution to the firm's profits. Basically, every producer should be generating three times their $100k salary – $300k – to meet the *Rule of Three*.

Here's how it breaks down:

1. The first third covers salary.

2. The second third covers the overhead associated with the person.

3. The final third produces a 30% profit.

If we applied this rule to our low utilization attorney, we'd immediately recognize that he's just barely covering his salary, let alone covering the overhead or profit that should be attributable to him. In fact, by having this individual on board, the law firm is losing over $200k in revenues. That's unsustainable in a small or mid-size firm – and should be considered unacceptable in any size firm.

THE *RULE OF THREE* IN CONTINGENCY- AND FIXED-FEE FIRMS

If you're a contingency attorney and wondering how any of this applies to your firm – trust us, it does. Figuring the cost of productive hours is difficult in firms that don't record time. But the *Rule of Three* can still be used to assess a producer's effectiveness in paying for themselves, their overhead costs and producing a profit. If your producers are meeting this rule, that means retaining them makes good sense from a financial perspective. In fact, because of the huge settlements and verdicts that can sometimes occur in many litigation practices, producers in Personal Injury and some other litigation firms have the best chance of exceeding the *Rule of Three* and producing levels of profit well beyond the 30% expected in other firms.

To analyze the productivity of contingency- and fixed-fee firm teams, you must first figure out how much revenue the producer and their team should generate per year. Teams produce that revenue jointly, so they must be considered a unit when they work to meet their revenue targets. Add up the salaries of each person who's dedicated to the team and multiply that sum by three to meet the *Rule of Three*. Since there are sometimes three to five people per team, this will be a sizeable number. If a person or persons are only partially dedicated to a team, reduce their salary amount to be roughly proportionate with the level of their contribution. To complete your productivity analysis, look at what the producer and team generated historically in the last several years and see how it compares to the *Rule of Three* goal.

Once you've multiplied all the relevant salaries by three, you know what the team should produce for the year. If you break that number down into monthly or quarterly revenue goals, you have the short-term productivity metrics that you can use to get the team to meet their yearly revenue goal.

For example:

If a team generates $500k per year, divide that by 4 to arrive at $125k per quarter. Divide that by 3 to get a monthly target of $41,666.

By meeting with the team monthly and comparing their actual revenue to their targeted amount, the team knows when they're off track. This allows them time to course-correct before the end of the quarter. It would be a mistake to let them arrive at the end of the quarter unaware that they're falling short. Depending on the kind of practice you're in, there may be a long lag time to deal with because your cases take a long time to resolve, so adjust accordingly. In some PI firms, they use their average fee-per-file to figure out the approximate number of demand letters they need to send per week to generate the revenue for each team. Then this becomes the metric they focus on as an interim measure, knowing that the money will follow.

In any case, if your firm is arranged in pods or teams, make sure each team knows how well the other is doing by setting up a scoreboard. This can create a little healthy competition if done in the right spirit.

If you are not dealing with production teams, just individuals in a contingency- or fixed-fee firm, their productivity is easy to track by comparing their collected revenues to their expected revenue targets on a regular basis. One advantage contingency-fee firms have is that they'll generally have a pretty high realization rate because of how they're paid; so a low utilization rate does not get further corrupted by low collections – just slow collections, as we explained earlier.

If your firm has fixed-fee and menu-based billing, you can require your team members to capture their time anyway. Many firms do this. That way, you have documentation of the time and effort that was spent on the client's behalf. You will be able to provide a judge with details in case you need to defend your fees, and you get valuable insight into the daily productivity of your team.

WHAT'S THE PROBLEM?

Now that we have various measures to track and analyze utilization and productivity, we have to identify why it's currently so low for so many. This is a multi-faceted problem. There are many factors that erode the productivity of your team. Some are more readily apparent than others. Lack of management oversight is the main problem, exacerbated by a failure to set productivity standards. Add to that bad time-capture habits on the part of the team, poor time-management habits all around, job description drift, plus a lack of proper delegation, and a bad situation becomes worse.

The good news is that all these problems can be fixed. It will take focus and diligent follow-through on the part of firm management, but, with a little work, you can begin to benefit from a team that is focused, fulfills their role as revenue producers, and starts generating a real profit. Let's explore how to make that happen.

You Can't Manage What You Don't Measure

Now that you know about utilization and the importance of this key management metric, you must measure it and manage it using either the billable-hours metric or revenue targets that fit the *Rule of Three*, as we just described.

For billable-hour firms, make it a rule that every timekeeper needs to report their time contemporaneously and finalize it on a weekly basis, whether that's in writing or captured in your billing software. If you need to train and retrain the team to use your software to track time, it's a worthy effort. Meet with the timekeepers at the end of every week to review their numbers. This meeting presents an opportunity to praise their success, and just knowing that they have to account to you at the end of the week will be a motivating force. If there are roadblocks, find out what they are and help clear them. Management's job is to make it easy for their people to hit their goals.

The method for holding contingency- and fixed-fee firms accountable is easier: Hold a monthly or quarterly meeting to see if they're hitting their interim revenue targets and are on track for their annual goal. Lavish them with praise if they are; if they're not, ask what obstacles are in their way. Then do your best to help them clear those obstacles.

Create Productivity Standards

In an hourly-billing firm, set up daily, weekly and monthly billing targets that will add up to an annual number that's appropriate for each producer. Track these targets consistently and set up a bonus system for exceeding them. If you've never had billing goals in your firm, we suggest you break them down to daily increments. It's more manageable for a team member to focus on being productive every day for a certain amount of time. Also, ensure that their time is being kept contemporaneously as much as possible, as that will maximize the time they capture. Don't let a pay period pass without checking in on the time that is posted. If someone is being careless about entering their time, have them speak to a supervising attorney every week. Some firms discuss their hours entered at every team meeting, and even publish the hours captured per person in a report given to the whole team.

Using a 50-week year (adjust this number to fit the typical amount of time off you give each position in your firm), here are some guidelines for hourly-billing firms:

1. **Legal secretaries** should be billing two to four hours per day, which works out to 500 to 1,000 hours a year.

2. **Paralegals** should bill from three to seven hours a day for 750 to 1,750 hours per year, depending on how well they're trained.

3. **Associates in their first three years** need to bill at least three to five hours a day, which is 750 to 1,250 a year.

4. **Experienced associates** need to bill five to eight hours daily for 1,250 to 2,000 hours a year.

Before you cast these goals in stone, discuss them with the team. Their input is important to hear before you get their buy-in. You may have to redistribute some of the administrative work they're doing (more about that later). Also, using a three-month ramp-up can help you evaluate and educate your staff as they step up to the new standards – especially if they haven't acquired the discipline of capturing their time. It can be daunting for some team members and, fair warning, some may decide to leave rather than meet them. But, if you replace them with someone who faithfully records their time and meets their goals, they'll produce higher revenues. All-in-all, your team may be better off without them.

To help your team meet their new hourly goals, make a game of it. As we mentioned before, many firms give associates and paralegals rewards and bonuses for hitting their goals. These include monetary and non-monetary rewards. Some firms let team members who hit their goals leave early on Fridays – a creative and surprisingly effective motivator. Other firms give a pre-set dollar amount as a bonus when their timekeepers meet their hourly targets. Alternatively, some firms award a percentage of the revenues for attorneys that come in after the hourly target is met.

RECORDING TIME IS AN ACQUIRED HABIT

Recording time, unfortunately, is a discipline that is best acquired early on. Hiring associates and paralegals who have worked in firms where they're required to capture their time from the start tend to be the best at it.

Many timekeepers post fewer hours because they simply forget to record it as legitimate work. This is typical for producers who try to acquire this habit later in life. As we've said, most firms today have software equipped with timekeeping functions that make capturing time as easy as possible. Using the time-capture function in your firm's software, and recording the time as contemporaneously as possible, is the standard everyone should eventually meet. Software providers are already devising ways, using a form of artificial intelligence, to help people capture their time better. In fact, some software manufacturers are already including a "predictive" time-capture function that anticipates how much time is spent on different tasks and proactively suggests it. So, this function will get easier in the future. But for now, if someone is new to recording their time and puts it on a legal pad to start with – it's better than nothing. From there, with constant reinforcement, try to get them to use the recording function in your software. If you happen to have a timekeeper who excels at recording their time, let them train the ones who struggle with it. They often have great tips and techniques to share.

A slightly more invasive solution is offered by the makers of Activtrak and Hubstaff, which, as of this writing, are software systems installed on company computers. This approach is not for everyone, but is certainly growing in popularity as more employees work virtually. It tracks keystrokes and takes screenshots at set intervals and ranks employee performance on a Dashboard.

THE TIME COP

For the more difficult cases, you may need to elect a person we call a Time Cop. It is this person's responsibility to check in on those who don't capture their time well – once in the morning, before lunch, once in the afternoon and then at the end of the day. This sounds like a lot of trouble, but think about all the revenue that's lost due to their failure to capture their time. As this person checks in with the struggling team members, they can either ask the person to stop what they're doing and input their time, or they can create a timesheet for that person by jotting down the time they think the person is putting in, capturing the client's name, and the type of task as well. Notes can then be compared at the end of the day. This sounds like an extreme measure, but, in an hourly-billing firm, the main thing sold is time. It takes time to get clients the outcome they seek. It takes time to do research, set strategy and prepare documents. Anyone on the team (that you'd like to keep around) who doesn't embrace this notion may require extra encouragement to do their part. Though some of the biggest offenders we see are recalcitrant team members, we've also encountered a lot of partners who are bad at capturing all their time. Using a Time Cop who is friendly but firm can help to bridge the gap while these individuals acquire the new habit.

BETTER TIME MANAGEMENT HABITS

Like every American, your team members are distracted and unfocused. Their attention span is only a few minutes long because they are interrupted – or interrupting themselves – constantly. The temptation to multi-task, check social media, shop on Amazon or text friends is almost irresistible, and the younger they are, the more they're addicted to constant interruption. This state of distraction does not lead to an error-free work product. To better understand this issue, check the updated excerpt on dealing with interruptions, which has been taken from our *Time Management* book. The excerpt has been included in Appendix #2.

JOB DESCRIPTION DRIFT

In the course of advising thousands of attorneys, we've seen firm management sabotage their own firm's ability to make a profit because their producers are loaded with tasks that could easily be done by non-revenue producers or less valuable players. If you or your firm is doing this, reconsider this approach immediately. Each of your associates (and their paralegals), should be viewed as profit centers, and every effort should be made to help them be as productive and profitable as possible.

In our previous example, remember how much revenue the "high-utilization" attorney generated compared to today's average attorney who clocks in at 31% utilization? And then, due to poor realization rates, the firm ultimately collects only 1.7 hours a day? Sometimes, this happens because the revenue producers have been asked to focus on things other than productive work. The producer who is overly burdened with lower-level tasks, such as clerical or receptionist-type duties, is being sabotaged by management.

Your associates, and many of your paralegals (depending on how you're organized), are the cashflow engine of your firm. Start treating them that way.

In fact, if you focus your producers on generating revenue, the dollars they bring in will more than pay for additional staff. If your producers could generate 1/3 to 1/2 again more revenue, this will more than pay for an assistant to whom they could delegate. This helps to maximize the profitability of the timekeeper. It's generally smarter to hire a less-expensive, lower-level employee to off-load work to, than to add additional producers. You can even hire "virtual" or contract staff members on a part-time basis so you don't have to add to your overhead costs. Sit down with each direct revenue producer and evaluate how much time they're spending on certain kinds of tasks. When you discover that they're overburdened with administrative tasks, help them off-load this non-revenue-producing work to someone else.

Managerial, marketing and administrative expectations should increase as certain associates approach partnership level – but, in order to be profitable, most of your younger associates should be workhorses.

IMPROVE DELEGATION AND PUSH WORK DOWN TO THE LOWEST LEVEL

Sometimes, when working with firms, we find that partners, associates and some team members are doing productive work, but it's well below their level of expertise. We believe all revenue producers should focus on the highest and best use of their time. If the associates can off-load productive work to a paralegal, they need to do so. If the paralegal is highly trained and capable of doing higher-level work, they should delegate down even further, to a legal secretary or clerical person. According to the *National Association of Legal Assistants 2016 National Compensation and Utilization Survey Report,* the trend toward increasing the duties and responsibilities of paralegals and legal assistants has been on the rise, which is a strong indication that these team members are steadily taking on more work.[2]

TRAIN YOUR STAFF TO UNDERSTAND TASKS AND TIMES

You may need to tighten your standards if you're in an hourly-billing firm, and your employees are consistently charging too much or too little for accomplishing certain tasks. Every firm is different, so what was considered an acceptable amount of time at a previous firm may not be acceptable to you. To make sure long-term team members and new hires are all on the same page, do what many of our attorney clients do and hold an office-wide billing seminar. Use this opportunity to resolve any confusion and focus on two concepts:

1. **What is and what isn't billable:** It's possible your team members are not charging for tasks that are legitimately chargeable. Even partner-level attorneys have questions about this, and it pays for you to sit down and distinguish this for your team. Less experienced team members will be particularly confused about what is billable and what is not. If you have checklists that dictate all the activities within your files, print them out and use them to identify and discuss what's billable and what's not. This will prevent the team from unknowingly giving away their time for free. A timekeeper's ignorance of this information can cause the firm to lose substantial fees.

2. **Time Expenditure Standards:** Work with your team to standardize how much time they can reasonably spend on different tasks. This is especially important if you notice certain team members consistently over- or under-billing for certain tasks. If they were given some standards or guidelines (i.e., "This should take between one and two hours," or "Expect to spend four hours on this," or "Talk to me if this takes you longer than three hours"), it would reduce the amount of time that has to be adjusted on the bills – barring unforeseen complications or special circumstances. They'd have a better idea of how to apply

their time more appropriately, which should result in faster bill review and fewer last-minute adjustments.

When your team members are trying to acquire new habits, like the ones we're discussing, using praise to reinforce their success is very important. Increasing their utilization rates by focusing the team on higher levels of production, learning to better capture their time, or tracking the revenues they're responsible for generating is mentally challenging work. Team members at all levels want and need recognition for these efforts. Positive feedback affirmation from supervisors is especially important when their team members are trying to transition to new habits and getting used to being held to higher levels of accountability. We've seen many situations in which team members fail to make this transition and leave. Typically, it's for the best, but it can still be disruptive.

If you're determined to create a financially healthy firm, instituting the kinds of changes discussed in this chapter are critical. Most of you, no matter how you bill, have not been taught about utilization, and your teams have been chronically underperforming for years. If that's true for you, you've left a lot of money on the table, but don't spend too much time looking back and agonizing about this. Most firms go through this phase because law schools don't train attorneys to be good business people. Focus instead on the many improvements you can make going forward.

COMPOUNDING EFFECTS MAKE MAGIC HAPPEN

When you re-engineer your utilization rate and combine this with, say, a rate raise, magic happens. Actually, profitability happens. Most of you don't have to hire more people to make more money – you just have to more fully utilize the ones you've got. The following is an example of what can happen when a firm begins to apply the first couple of **RULES** that we've discussed so far. We'll use the example of a firm of 25 attorneys that we worked with recently. Their average billing rate was $150 an hour and they billed an average of 1600 hours a year. We asked them to do two things:

Increase their hours billed by one hour a month, per attorney.

Increase their average billing rate by 5%, from $150 to $157.50.

These two seemingly small actions combined to generate an additional $302,250 in revenue for the firm. Again, we only asked their attorneys to bill one extra hour a month! Then we asked the firm to raise rates by 5%, which was a tiny increase of $7.50 per hour. Neither of these actions are huge, yet they amplified each other to generate an impressive amount of revenue. And since there was very little expense involved to generate this revenue, it substantially increased the firm's profitability.

Hopefully, this example helps you see that each of the concepts in the **RULES** builds on and amplifies each other – with impressive results. In the next chapter, we'll talk about leverage, which is only possible when you maintain healthy levels of utilization. It's another strategy you can use to take your firm to the next level of profitability.

IMPACT OF BILLING INCREASES ON REVENUES

Assumptions:	
25 attorneys Average billing rate: $150/hour Average billing hours per year = 1,600	
Billing hours/attorney	**Billing rate**
Increase average number of billing hours per month per attorney by 1 hour	Increase average billing rate by 5% to $157.50
300 hours a year at $150 = $45,000	$7.50 times 40,000 hours = $300,000
Combined: 40,300 hours a year with an additional $7.50 an hour increase, nets the firm a $302,250 gain.	

ENDNOTES

1

Clio's 2019 Legal Trends Report,
www.clio.com/legal-trends/2019-report

2

National Association of Legal Assistants 2016 National
Compensation and Utilization Survey Report

Chapter 4

LEVERAGE

How To Build Profit-Centered Teams

"Unfortunately, your firm is upside-down," said Senior Atticus Practice Advisor Glenn Finch, in day two of one of our Practice Growth Program workshops. He started drawing a pyramid. "Let me make this simple. The ideal firm is pyramid-shaped: Smaller at the top and larger at the bottom." Pointing to his drawing he asked, "You have five partners? And three associates supported by two paralegals?"

The client, we'll call him Phillip, nodded in confirmation. "That's right. We handle Real Estate, Estate Planning, Probate and Estate Administration." His firm had ramped up their marketing efforts since they joined the program. Now, business was booming and they were overwhelmed. Their success had surfaced some underlying inefficiencies – in this case, how poorly they were structured.

"You've got an inverted pyramid structure. The exact opposite of how your firm should be structured for profitability," Glenn commented as he put down the marker. "Today we're going to talk about leverage, Phillip. This concept can and will turn things around for you and your firm, in terms of production and profitability." Speaking to the whole group, he said, "Phillip is generously allowing us to critique how his firm is structured, but he's not alone. I know many of you are dealing with this same issue." He paused for a moment. "Consider this – lawyers are *over-qualified* for most of the work that goes into the average case, file or matter – regardless of what your practice area may be. To maximize profitability, you need to organize your firm around that fact."

A few heads nodded in agreement, but some looked unconvinced. He continued, "**Leverage** is the **"L"** in the **RULES** we've been discussing. To best explain it, I want you to think back. At some point, you had to take physics. And you learned how a large object, say a heavy boulder, could be moved by a lightweight person using a bar and a fulcrum to multiply their strength. Without leverage, the person's power and strength were limited. The lever mechanically amplified their output."

"In the law firm, leverage is best thought of as the number of revenue producers per partner. On their own, partners have limited output, which caps the amount of revenue they can produce. But that output is multiplied by the associates, paralegals and legal assistants to whom the partner can delegate. The bigger the team, the greater the leverage. And with greater leverage comes greater profitability."

Understanding Leverage

Like many attorneys, Phillip's firm had grown organically when he and several of his colleagues – all refugees from large firms – decided to join forces. In our experience, attorneys who experience leverage as young associates working for large firms frequently come away with a negative view of the concept. Toiling away at the bottom of the pyramid, they knew they were being used to generate revenue, but probably didn't appreciate much more than that. It left them vowing that if they ever opened their own firms, they'd never make *their* teams work that hard.

We believe you don't have to be a slave-driver to make a profit, and that it's possible to set up almost any firm to be productive and profitable without killing your team with unrealistic hourly requirements. First, the firm must be structured with an emphasis on how each partner sets up the teams they supervise. These teams must be designed to be profit centers. The second step involves distributing the work in each file to maximize profit margins, and the third focuses on how all of this is amplified by the right technology.

THREE STRATEGIES TO MAXIMIZE LEVERAGE

Let's examine these steps in depth to learn how they work and how you can measure their effectiveness. First, we'll define the strategy, then we'll give you a Key Performance Indicator to help you measure it.

1. **Organize your firm around Profit Centers,** according to *Leveraging with Legal Assistants,* by Arthur Greene. Each partner should be leveraged with a profit-producing team. To be properly leveraged, he or she should not be the biggest producer on the team. Instead, they should be supported by the right mix of associates, paralegals and legal assistants specific to the practice area. This hierarchy greatly amplifies the revenue each partner can generate because the work continually gets pushed down to the *most competent but least expensive* person. The number of teams working with each partner is limited only by the partner's ability to manage and supervise them. We typically see one to three teams per partner, but sometimes see more.[1]

   Key Performance Indicator: The *Rule of Three.* Your Profit Centers should generate three times their combined salaries on an annual basis.

   Note: If a team member only participates part time because they're assigned to other work as well, back out a proportionate amount of their salary.

2. **Maximize profit on a per-file basis.** Profitability on a per-file basis is dependent on shifting large portions of work to lower-paid, but well-trained associates, paralegals and legal assistants to keep the cost of production as low as possible relative to the fees received. Highly routinized, forms-driven practice areas are the best fit for this strategy. Typically, the more complex the file, the more attorney involvement is needed. Also important here is a reminder that hourly-billing firms should consider moving to flat fees in this case.

> **Key Performance Indicator:** Track percent of attorney time to staff time per file. As a general rule, reducing attorney hours and increasing assistant hours creates more profitability per file.[2]

3. **Use technology to increase efficiencies and streamline processes.** Prior to the introduction of case management software, producing leverage was limited to adding more people to a team. With the advent of this software, that situation is no longer true. For many practice areas, increased efficiency means that a file is processed faster, allowing more files to be processed in the course of a year.

> **Key Performance Indicator:** Time On Desk. We find, typically, this is gauged by how long it takes a matter to get through the pipeline – from when it's opened to when it's closed. Your case management software can help speed up this process and allows one person to expand their capacity to do more work. The exception to this emphasis on speed occurs in PI and other litigation firms where it's important to take more time to develop higher-value cases. In all practice areas, the focus on speed must not pull down the average fee-per-file, which tells you the quality of the cases being accepted.

THE DIVISION OF LABOR: PARTNERS

Now that we've given you the overview of the three best ways to improve your leverage, let's focus a little more on how to structure your teams to enhance profitability. These teams are organized on the philosophy that attorneys are, as we've mentioned, overqualified to do most of the work in any given case, file or matter. This is true for most firms, except for those rare, deeply-niched, specialty firms based on a lone attorney's expertise. For the overwhelming majority of firms, profit-centered teams are led by a higher-priced lawyer who sets strategy, gives direction and supervises all activities. Partners and some senior associates occupy these top positions, and they should focus on those activities generally considered to be the practice of law, including:

> *Accepting a case; setting fees; evaluating a case and charting its course; performing legal analysis; giving legal advice; participating in the formal judicial process (depositions, hearings, trials, etc.); supervising legal assistants .*[3]

Since those tasks represent a small percentage of the work to be done, the rest of the team should be staffed with highly-trained but less expensive talent. Associates fall into this category and can obviously do attorney-level work; in areas with a glut of newly-minted attorneys but few paralegals, new attorneys are often found in paralegal roles. But setting them aside, paralegals and legal assistants typically make up the rest of the team, because the objective is to push work down to the least expensive person and free up the partners to supervise more files, in addition to marketing and managing the firm. Consequently, we recommend partners restrict their personal production to four or five hours a day, whenever possible.

Having said that, we don't want you to skimp on the level of service you provide your clients. In fact, having great assistants on your team can actually enhance delivery times and client communication, which directly impact client satisfaction. Our goal is to get you to deliver excellent service in the most efficient and economical way possible – and that usually involves the extensive use of well-trained paralegals and legal assistants.

It's worth pausing for a moment to consider the advantages of working with these individuals. In his book, Greene points out that not only are these para-professionals less expensive, they're typically more humble, easier to work with and – best of all – they won't expect to become a partner one day. Compare that to the entitled young associates out there who expect to be on a partner track almost immediately and will jump ship to get there after you've invested time in training them. This is not to say that paralegals and legal assistants will never leave. They will. But they'll never steal your clients the way an ambitious associate will.[4]

To be clear, we're not against hiring associates; many firms must hire them, especially because paralegals and legal assistants can't appear in court. And by hiring right, there are ways to mitigate the risks associated with hiring them as part of your team. We just want to underscore the wisdom – and enhanced profitability – of using para-professionals whenever possible.

As you consider re-engineering your firm to be more profitable, you'll probably need to add more paralegals and/or legal assistants. Keep in mind: The right paralegal or legal assistant must possess qualities beyond what their training and experience will give them. The right personality is critical to their success. As communicators, they need to strike the right tone in order to inspire confidence when they interact with both clients and other attorneys. As representatives of your firm, they must project a personable yet professional manner in the way they present themselves.

THE DIVISION OF LABOR:
PARALEGALS AND LEGAL ASSISTANTS

Back to the division of labor we were discussing. We identified the tasks that specifically make up the practice of law. They're the most critical, even though they may represent only 10% to 20% of the time spent on any given case. This is where the supervising attorney or partner should focus their time for maximum impact. Next, we'll describe what assistants can and cannot do under their supervision. We're taking the time to clarify these tasks because many attorneys and team members are confused about where to draw the line. That lack of clarity may lead some attorneys to limit what their paralegals and legal assistants can do to support them. These are assistant-level tasks:

> *Obtaining facts from a client; communicating information to clients; preparing drafts of documents; interviewing witnesses; performing limited legal research to assist the lawyer with the legal analysis; preparing drafts of memos, letters, orders, pleadings, forms; answering telephones; greeting clients; supporting clients; obtaining documents and photographs; preparing summaries and chronologies; preparing itemization of claims, interrogatories and production requests; preparing drafts of responses to discovery requests; preparing outlines for attorneys to use in deposing witnesses; indexing deposition transcripts; preparing summaries of the evidence; preparing exhibit lists.*[5]

Clearly, the list of what well-trained paralegals and legal assistants can do to support attorneys is extensive, yet many attorneys fail to take advantage of the full scope of what they can do. Use this list as a reference when setting up and training your teams to support the work of the lawyer.

LET'S DO THE MATH

Let's do some easy math to illustrate the importance of delegating to assistants, and show the real impact of leverage at work. In this first scenario, the attorney is like Phillip, who you met at the beginning of this chapter. The way his firm is organized, he's doing most of the work himself, with a small amount of help from his legal assistant. In this example, they're working on a large case, with Phillip doing the bulk of the work. The breakdown of labor and associated costs adds up like this:

The attorney bills 40 hours at $200 = $8,000
The assistant bills 10 hours at $75 = $ 750
_____

The total fee is = $8,750

Compare it to this next scenario, using the same case and same hourly rates, but this time shifting more work to the assistant instead of the attorney:

The attorney bills 16 hours at $200 = $3,200
The assistant bills 34 hours at $75 = $2,550
_____

The total fee is = $5,750

Not surprisingly, the fee, after the work has been redistributed, is substantially lower, with a reduction in cost to the client from $8,750 to $5,750. This is a cost savings of $3,000 to the client. But this fee reduction actually opens up an opportunity: What would happen if the attorney raised his rates in this scenario?[4] Let's take a look:

The attorney bills 16 hours at $300 = $4,800
The assistant bills 34 hours at $75 = $2,550

The total fee is = $7,350

In this case, we've maintained a significantly lower cost to the client, even though we've raised the lawyer's fee by $100 an hour!

But that's not all. By shifting a larger portion of the work to legal assistants, the lawyer can now generate more revenue overall. If he moves from billing $200 to $300 an hour, but still bills his standard 1500 hours a year, he generates an additional $150,000 in annual revenue. In fact, he could decrease his hours to be more in line with what we recommend, and still see an increase. We discussed the power of a rate raise earlier in this book, but, in this example, the raise occurs without the client feeling the pinch because the overall fee is lower.

Secondly, by shifting more work to his assistants, the attorney can handle a greater volume of files. Using our sample file as an example, at 40 hours per file, he could only handle 37 files a year. At 16 hours per file, he could handle 93 files per year. That's an impressive **increase of approximately 250%** in terms of output.

Taken together, the compounding effect of dividing the labor differently on a per-file basis, combined with a rate raise for the attorney, is dramatic. The lawyer is now able to handle an increased volume of files at an increased rate – and the client pays less! You might not be able to duplicate these exact results given the type of work you do, but go through this exercise to see how it plays out in your own practice.[6]

Don't Be A Hero

Now that you understand how to divide the labor in your teams, you must set them up to best serve the kinds of cases you do. Some teams, because of the cases they handle, will be more attorney-intensive, and some will be more staff-intensive. It's up to you to decide what's the best fit for the kind of work you do.

One attorney-intensive configuration reflects what we call the "Heroic" leadership style. Seen frequently in those firms where the partners are the biggest producers on their teams, this intense approach in their firms not only leads to early burn-out, it also stunts the firm's growth because vital activities like marketing and managing get neglected. We recommend partners limit their production to no more than four or five hours a day.

Not Everyone Is Partnership Material

Furthermore, most small to mid-sized firms shouldn't offer unlimited partnership opportunities to their associates. This opens the door to too many "service partners," who may be brilliant technicians and big producers, but only work on production and don't help with the marketing and/or managerial burdens of leadership. This was the case in Phillip's firm, which was basically a group of colleagues sharing office space but lacking central leadership. For more typical firms, creating a two- or three-tiered partnership structure may be helpful as a way to confer status and higher-level bonuses on senior associates who are workhorses (non-equity partnerships with limited voting rights and no distributions), while keeping the top tier restricted to triple-threat talent (those who can find it, mind it and grind it). These individuals should be allowed a seat at the table because they understand how to leverage themselves.

Firms should establish a well-defined set of escalating standards for partnership that their associates can follow, and they should be rigorous about enforcing them at every step along the path. In addition, there should be a capital investment requirement (this can be accomplished by withholding part of a person's salary over time if they don't have a lump sum to invest). Having rigorous standards and requiring a capital investment ensures that the upper ranks stay small (remember the pyramid shape), concentrates the profit at the top, and helps develop serious contenders for succession.

Below are brief explanations, excerpted from our book *Hire Slow, Fire Fast,* of different law firm models which you may find helpful when building or re-engineering your firm to maximize your margins.

THE VERTICAL SILO MODEL

Typically, the workhorse team in a small firm is composed of a partner-level attorney paired with an associate, and/or a paralegal with a legal assistant. Sometimes there are several associates, paralegals and legal assistant pods assigned to one attorney; it depends largely upon how much work the partner can generate and manage. If the partner can generate a large amount of work, they may have several associates and paralegal teams who handle the work. No matter how many are on the team, or how many sub-teams are created, these are vertical silos, and each one works exclusively for their supervising partner. In a firm with several partners, each partner would have their own practice group, and, except for some situations, there would be little cross-utilization between the teams. These kinds of arrangements allow team members to become very efficient because they are continually dealing with variations of the same kinds of matters, files or cases. People tend to get better and faster at things they do repetitively, which argues against hourly billing because it penalizes speed. In situations like this, a switch to flat-fee or menu-based billing will maximize profitability.

THE ATTORNEY/CASE MANAGER SILO MODEL

In many PI firms, the team is led by the partner or supervising attorney, with a case manager directly below them. The case manager may be an attorney, but often (because they are less expensive), they are highly-experienced, energetic and well-organized senior paralegals who supervise the activity on each case matter or file to ensure deadlines are met, clients are served, and production is progressing. In this model, the case manager will oversee the work of the associates and paralegals who are a part of the partner's team. This remains a "silo" model since the teams serve one partner, not multiple partners. And, like the first example, a team such as this tends to develop a great deal of subject matter knowledge because their focus is limited.

In PI firms of any size, you'll often find a two-tier system with some teams working on cases that will likely settle (the "pre-lit" teams), housed next to and separate from litigation teams focused on higher-value cases deemed likely to go to trial. This division of labor allows each team to develop expertise at what they do, and it usually means they increase their effectiveness. The fact that the firm tries cases and is not just a settlement firm tends to raise the average fee-per-file across the board.

THE ATTORNEY/PARALEGAL SILO MODEL

In practice areas that are forms-driven and highly delegable, many partner-level attorneys rely on highly-experienced paralegals and legal assistants to assist them, foregoing using associates altogether. This approach won't work for everyone, but for forms-driven practice areas such as Real Estate, Estate Planning and Elder Law (those practice areas that can either find highly-trained paralegals, or train them from scratch), this model has the potential to deliver the highest level of profitability. As we've stated before, that's magnified even further when the firm abandons hourly billing (penalizing speed and efficiency), and converts to menu-based billing.

THE LABOR POOL MODEL

In this model, firms made up of multiple partners delegate to a pool of associates and/or paralegals and legal assistants. The work is delegated based on who has the requisite skills and available capacity at the time. There are no pre-set, specialized, vertical teams in place. For this model to work and be effective, all the associates and paralegals must be trained in all relevant practice areas so they consistently can be cross-utilized by all the partners. This model best serves a firm made up of partners who focus on practice areas which have seasonal shifts or spikes in production due to varying business cycles. It also works well when a firm's practice areas are complementary, such as Estate Planning and Elder Law. Where the types of law are related, this makes sense. It is more difficult, however, for the team members to develop real expertise and depth when they are dealing with widely disparate areas of the law. When that happens, efficiency suffers and Time On Desk increases. This arrangement doesn't offer the same advantages as the others because of the constantly shifting nature of the work, but it does increase profitability to a degree because work is being pushed down to the least expensive level of competency and not being handled just by an attorney.

DELEGATION IS KEY

The common thread that runs through all these models is their ability to leverage the lawyers at the top of the pyramid. But this emphasis on leverage can be difficult to maintain over time. It is our experience that most attorneys embrace the idea in theory, but stray from the concept after they've had a few bad experiences with delegation. If, for example, they've become embarrassed because an assignment they delegated to an associate didn't get done and affected the outcome of a client's case, their trust for that team member degrades. And when they develop a lack of trust for their team, be they associates, paralegals or legal assistants, they will start to hold on to work that could *and should* be delegated.

They justify this by telling themselves that they can't produce the desired result for the client without doing most of the work themselves. Instead of providing better oversight, they hoard the work and become bottlenecks in the process. Desks piled high with files are the sign of someone who isn't pushing the work to the next person in line. Unfortunately, as this person's ability to leverage themselves declines, so does their profitability because they can work on only a limited number of files.

We've seen that a lack of trust leading to a lack of delegation can happen anywhere down the line. It is not restricted to partners or associates, and is found in paralegals, legal secretaries and so on. Be on the lookout for signs (i.e., piles of files, unless it's a paperless office) that you or members of your team have started hoarding work, in order to re-establish better delegation habits.

WEEKLY CASE STATUS MEETING

To help supervising attorneys improve supervision and keep the flow of work moving, we recommend they hold a weekly meeting in which all the cases they're overseeing are discussed. We call this a Weekly Case Status Meeting. Basically, this is the supervising attorney's opportunity to sit down with the team, review each case, strategize if needed, and discuss the next steps. This meeting is very effective at keeping the cases moving, and shortens their Time On Desk. As you know, we recommend that the financial status of the case also be reviewed at this meeting. Doing so prevents the team from investing huge chunks of time in cases where the client is no longer paying (this helps keep your realization rate high). Meetings like these not only result in the cases being worked properly and moving more swiftly; they give peace of mind to the supervising attorney *and* the team because fewer items fall through the cracks with this protocol.

THE DILEMMA FOR HOURLY-BILLING FIRMS

Unfortunately, while the redistribution of labor benefits the partners in an hourly-billing firm, the total overall fees to the firm are reduced when legal assistants take over the bulk of the work. If you're in a highly competitive market and you must compete on price – that's great. Unfortunately, for the rest, **"hourly billing rewards inefficiency"** has kicked in and now your average fee-per-file has gone down. This means the profit-per-file is less, even though the capacity of the partner has been increased.

If you're an hourly biller and your average fee-per-file suffers when you redistribute the labor in your files, consider a move to flat-fee or menu-based billing (even if you allow some hourly billing for work that exceeds the normal scope), as we've covered previously in this book. The calculations we've previously discussed – figuring out the optimal ratio of attorney hours to staff hours in each kind of case you typically handle, then adding up the costs – are the same calculations you'd do to set a flat fee. Just remember to build in a profit margin on top of your costs.

LEVERAGING WITH TECHNOLOGY

The last but not least way to amplify the effects of leverage is to use case management software. We've just explored staffing your teams in favor of creating more profitability, and then we looked at how to maximize your profit on a per-file basis. But there are more efficiencies to be gained. One more way to gain leverage is through the use of technology.

We recommend you use case management software if you want to streamline your operation, optimize your productivity and eliminate the paper chase. Most systems provide your firm with a centralized platform for all the critical functions that would otherwise be separate.

- **Managing and creating documents**
- **Calendaring**
- **Client communication**
- **Data collection**
- **Time tracking**
- **Billing**

Some platforms allow you to customize your workflows and automate a variety of different processes to fit your individual preferences. In addition to these capabilities, some feature Customer Relationship Management (CRM) functions to support your marketing efforts.

When it comes to matter management, this kind of software makes it easier for the supervising attorney to keep track of everything they are overseeing. Now they can assign tasks and track their completion; access the status of a case with the push of a button; track its progress; and be alerted about upcoming deadlines. This gives partners and supervising attorneys all the right tools to expand what they can accurately oversee and manage. And, as their ability to manage more cases grows, their profitability grows.

We still recommend that the supervising attorney conduct their Weekly Case Status Meetings to discuss progress on each matter as it goes through the pipeline, but case management software can provide a great deal of information in a moment's notice.

Since technology evolves so quickly, we don't want to recommend certain software and have our choices rendered obsolete by the time this book goes to print. In the world of technology, if it's not current, it doesn't count. For the most up-to-date information, go online to a site called *Capterra (https://www.capterra.com/law-practice-management-software/)*. As of this writing, they've been around a while and have established a pretty good reputation. They regularly review and rank the year's best law practice management software. As you start your quest for the best software match, they can help point you in the right direction. Their robust search function enables you to search for the capabilities you want, the pricing options you'd prefer, and the features you can't live without.

In addition to online research, survey your colleagues for the case management software they most prefer. Then cross-check their recommendations with online reviews, and engage a consultant to help you make your final determination. Arriving at the perfect fit for your firm can be a big project, so delegating the initial research to a tech-savvy team member who understands your parameters can help. Instruct them to narrow the field to the top three picks, then get involved for the final selection. Though the search for the right software can be time-consuming, the payoff can be significant due to the time and effort it will save for years to come.

In Conclusion

In this chapter, we've looked at several ways to employ and then amplify the effects of leverage: creating teams that are profit centers; strategically redistributing the labor on a per-file basis; and using technology to speed up and streamline your most critical processes. Next, we'll look at another aspect of your firm's financial foundation which directly impacts your profitability: Your firm's expenses. If you think you know everything there is to know about this topic, read on. We're going to recommend a new strategy that changes everything.

ENDNOTES

1
Greene, Arthur G., (1993) Leveraging with Legal Assistants: How to Maximize Team Performance, Improve Quality, and Boost your Bottom Line, p.5

2
Greene, Arthur G., (1993) Leveraging with Legal Assistants: How to Maximize Team Performance, Improve Quality, and Boost your Bottom Line, p.9

3
Greene, Arthur G., (1993) Leveraging with Legal Assistants: How to Maximize Team Performance, Improve Quality, and Boost your Bottom Line, p.8

4
Greene, Arthur G., (1993) Leveraging with Legal Assistants: How to Maximize Team Performance, Improve Quality, and Boost your Bottom Line, p.16

5
Greene, Arthur G., (1993) Leveraging with Legal Assistants: How to Maximize Team Performance, Improve Quality, and Boost your Bottom Line, p.20

6
Greene, Arthur G., (1993) Leveraging with Legal Assistants: How to Maximize Team Performance, Improve Quality, and Boost your Bottom Line, p.15

Chapter 5

EXPENSES

What Are You Spending Your Money On?

"I'm very frugal. I keep a close eye on the firm's expenses and no one's authorized to spend anything out of the ordinary without talking to me first," said an attorney, we'll call him Andrew, who was the owner of a small firm with three partners. He stood up to share his philosophy about controlling expenses in one of our Practice Growth programs. Patrick Wilson, the facilitator, responded, "That's smart. Sounds like you have a good approval process when it comes to spending." He then asked, "Do you think controlling costs is the best way to produce a profit?" Andrew hesitated and then said, "Well, it's got to be important. So many firms don't keep track of what they're spending." Patrick agreed. "You're right. Controlling costs is important, but it's not the biggest contributor to profitability."

Andrew looked around the room, hoping to see some agreement among the other participants, and asked, "Are you saying we shouldn't pay attention to our expenses?"

"Absolutely not," responded the facilitator. "In fact, it's vital to keep them low. We've just noticed, in working with hundreds of small firm attorneys, that they tend to over-emphasize this strategy as the only way to create profitability. For many lawyers, this is the only tool in their toolbox when it comes to creating a profit. We want to put it in its proper context with all the other levers that we've discussed."

He turned to the whiteboard and started writing. "Just to reiterate, if you don't use and follow the first three **RULES**, controlling costs won't be enough to create profitability. They all work together. It's a lot to keep track of, so here is a quick review of the first three.":

1. **Rates and Realization:** Setting the correct rates and keeping the realization rate at 95% and above

2. **Utilization Rate:** Making sure that the utilization rate of your timekeepers is kept high – 80% to 95% where possible

3. **Leverage:** Maximizing the capacity of the revenue producers on the team so they can handle a greater number of cases, files or clients

"Using these first three levers will get you to profitability faster than saving money on expenses – but saving money is still important. In fact, we're going to give you some guidelines for what's reasonable to spend," Patrick continued. "Then we'll introduce you to an exciting new philosophy that ties into the idea of minimizing expenses and helps you proactively build profitability by budgeting for it."

Then he said, "Speaking of budgets – raise your hand if you create and use a budget on an annual basis." A few hands went up and the rest of the group looked uncomfortable. One lawyer spoke up. "When I worked for a large firm, we went through a planning and budgeting process. It was a lot of work. I just don't have the time for it in my own firm."

RATIO GUIDELINES

Many of our clients don't create a budget because of the time involved. But we believe it's an important tool to help you manage your finances. For now, whether you use a budget or not, we're going to give you some spending guidelines to follow. They can help you assess where your expenses are out of line, especially for occupancy and overhead costs. Then you can work to bring your expenses in line and budget accordingly.

For many of our clients, these guidelines act as a bridge to the budgeting process. Even though the guidelines shift a little, depending on your location, the labor market and your specific practice areas, they can immediately indicate where you're overspending.

Here are the general guidelines:
- **People costs:** Staff, attorney salaries, insurance, taxes, 38%-42%
- **Occupancy costs:** Less than 10%, ideally 6%-8%
- **Equipment costs:** 3%-5%
- **Marketing costs:** 4%-7%
- **Miscellaneous:** CLE (Continuing Legal Education), consulting, travel, 3%-5%
- **Profit:** 30%-40%

Keep in mind these guidelines are approximate and won't always add up to 100% since they're expressed in ranges.

PEOPLE COSTS

The biggest expense in everyone's firm is your human capital; in other words, your people. Their salaries, health benefits, insurance and associated taxes are your biggest expense – by far. Expect to pay 38% to 42% of your revenue on your employees. On a national basis, larger firms may pay up to 67.6% for their people-related costs due to their location. Firms in competitive markets often decide to pay more generous salaries and provide enhanced benefits to retain team members and reduce turnover.[1]

Payroll and Benefits is the first area most firms consider when cutting costs, followed by Occupancy costs. These two areas make up your largest expenditures. However, until artificial intelligence replaces us all, you can't operate without a team. In fact, as we discussed at length in the chapter on Leverage, there is rarely a profit without a team. Take a look at the following suggestions to help you control and reduce your people-related costs:

1. **Assess performance levels and train.** Consistently assess your team and replace non-performers with people who have a record of productivity. Constantly train your team so they perform at high levels. To maximize their efficiency even further, keep them updated on how to use your firm's software.

2. **Hire paralegals and legal assistants over associates.** Use highly-trained non-lawyers at every opportunity. If you can't find them with the training they need, train them yourself. Hire associates sparingly, if possible. Constantly push work down to the most competent but least expensive person on the team. Don't have $300 an hour associates doing $75 an hour work. Also, don't have highly-trained paralegals doing clerical work. Keep your revenue producers free of administrative burdens to maximize their profitability.

3. **Build in flexibility.** To handle peak loads and seasonal needs, use virtual paralegals, online paralegal service providers, part-time assistants and associates, attorneys who are work-at-home contractors, and trusted temp agencies. Don't add permanent, long-term team members for short-term needs.

4. **Create controls around overtime authorization.** Be wary of those who accrue excessive overtime. It could be a legitimate sign that the person is overwhelmed and needs more time – or they may be padding their paycheck. Look into it.

5. **Outsource administrative tasks.** Doing this reduces the number of non-producers and their corresponding benefits. Candidates for outsourcing are payroll management, IT, messenger services and copier management.

6. **Control general staff expenses.** Don't eliminate group outings, firm meetings, firm retreats and partnership meetings if they are well planned and well executed. They help build morale and are justified when the costs are controlled, i.e., don't be extravagant in venue selection.

7. **Offer a Cafeteria Plan.** A Cafeteria Plan is an employee benefit plan that allows staff to choose from a variety of pre-tax benefits. A Cafeteria Plan is also called a "Flexible Benefit Plan," or a Section 125 plan. This may require additional administration (set them up, where possible, to allow changes on a limited basis), but they allow employees to customize what's right for their age and stage of life. And with no federal, state or Social Security taxes deducted, employees can potentially save between 25% to 40% of every dollar they contribute. This is perceived positively by team members and in some cases can save employers money. *(https://www.investopedia.com/terms/c/cafeteriaplan.asp).*

As we've mentioned, exceptions to these guidelines occur if there's a lot of competition for employees in your market. In that case, you might decide to overpay, or offer enhanced benefits to your paralegals and attorneys to keep them from jumping ship. This strategy could add up to be 10% to 20% over what these team members would receive elsewhere, but, for many firm owners, it's worth it. In many cases, they're making the right calculation: There's a lot to be said for keeping a happy, productive and well-trained team going, and minimizing the significant costs, lost time, training and hassles associated with turnover.

Another compensation issue involves how much partners/owners pay themselves. Some pay themselves at a much higher rate than it would cost to replace them. If you're a firm owner or shareholder, we recommend you pay yourself based on what it would cost to replace you for the work you do. Then take the rest of what's owed you in distributions. Before you do this, check to see if your CPA agrees with this advice for you and your situation. Usually, we find this to be a good tax strategy for firm owners and it's an important indicator that the owner/partners are not the biggest producers in their firms. Why is this important? They need to maximize their leverage with profit-centered teams so they can attend to the marketing, managerial and growth needs of the firm. As we've already emphasized, firms will stagnate if the partner is the biggest producer, and their revenues will suffer because their capacity is constrained.

OCCUPANCY COSTS

Occupancy costs can take up to 10% of your cashflow, but we recommend you keep them between 6% and 8%. These costs cover your building's rent or lease, electricity, plumbing, signage and office furnishings. We don't want you to skimp on anything that the client encounters; your front office furniture and décor should look good and be consistent with your brand. Always try to match your office and its décor to the level of clients you're trying to serve. You don't want your office to look cheap or shabby; it does not inspire trust and confidence in the eyes and minds of potential clients. Look for space that looks good but is not over-priced.

If you must expand your team and you're limited by your current lease to a small space, find creative solutions rather than incurring more expense by taking on a larger space. If you can't expand using discontinuous space in the building, explore using virtual workers, work-from-home contractors, team members who will share desks and offices, and those who might work a late shift. Do everything you can to control your costs here since it's your second biggest expenditure.

Exceptions to the 10% guideline might occur if you own your office space or building, and you charge yourself a high rent because of the tax advantages. Another exception might be the choice to move into a better building filled with existing and potential referral sources. In both cases, your occupancy costs will be higher, but the benefits should outweigh the expenses.

EQUIPMENT COSTS

Equipment costs encompass computers, internet and phone service, software rental or purchase, copy machines, and the coffee maker (and coffee) in the breakroom. There isn't a lot of wiggle room here, so expect these expenses to take up 3% to 5%. It's the cost of doing business. You may be able to reduce some of the people costs associated with some of the maintenance of this equipment by following our advice to outsource management of these tasks and reduce the number of administrators on your team.

MARKETING COSTS

Marketing expenses for small and mid-sized firms should be 4% to 7% of your annual revenues. For most practices, 4% to 7% is a good range – especially for small and mid-sized firms that focus primarily on referral marketing and may have a part-time or virtual marketing assistant.

These guidelines don't apply to attorneys who advertise heavily, especially on television and the internet. Their costs are much higher and depend on factors such as: who they're trying to reach; the size of their target market; how saturated with competitors these markets are; and the amount of reach they want. Their costs will also depend on pay-per-click rates and the expense of local media buys, which vary by location. Obviously, the larger the market, the more competition there will be and the more expensive the advertising will be.

Miscellaneous Costs

Miscellaneous costs include Continuing Legal Education (CLE) classes, consulting and Bar association fees, state fees, fees not re-imbursed by clients, travel, and whatever else doesn't easily fall into the other categories. Keep an eye on charges for your subscription research software. Firms should treat automated research tools as lawyer expenses for billing purposes, and spread expenses to clients when applicable. Firms shouldn't treat these charges as out-of-pocket expenses. Keep an eye on this, as competition to provide these services is heating up and prices are going down.

Many firms put their Professional Liability and other insurance here. Some classify them as operating expenses, along with state and local taxes, professional fees to accountants and other attorneys, and consultants. To save money, some firms increase their deductible, operate very conservatively, screen their clients wisely, and hope nothing will happen. But each firm must weigh their individual level of risk based on their practice areas, the types of services they provide and the types of clients they serve. The firm that focuses, for example, on medium-priced residential house closings versus those that do Securities and Exchange Commission work, is at a much lower level of risk.

Profit First Approach

To further support your chances of creating profitability, we suggest you take the approach advocated by Mike Michalowicz in his book *Profit First*. The approach he advocates turns the normal method of arriving at a profit on its head. The customary, or GAAP (Generally Accepted Accounting Principles) approach taken by most law firm owners and indeed most business owners, looks like this:

REVENUE – EXPENSES = PROFIT

This conventional approach means that whatever revenue is left over at the end of the year, after all the expenses have been deducted, is your profit.[2]

Instead of following the traditional thinking, the basic idea behind the *Profit First* philosophy is to reverse-engineer the way profit is accumulated. According to Michalowicz, instead of just accepting what's left at the end of the year as profit, a business should proactively budget for their profit – similar to how they'd save money for an anticipated expense. His philosophy proposes that the revised equation look like this:

REVENUE – PROFIT = EXPENSES

This means that when revenue comes into your firm on a monthly basis, you'd immediately set aside a predetermined percentage of that revenue for profit. For safekeeping, you'd hold that profit in a separate, designated account and watch it accumulate month after month, never withdrawing any of the funds for expenses. If, for example, you project a profit of $120k a year for your firm, you'd proactively put away $10k a month. The deposits into the profit account would look like this: $10k per month x 12 months = $120k profit.

In reality, most firm owners don't have the confidence or the cashflow to deposit the full $10k in the first month – or even the first quarter. They'd put in a lesser amount, say $5k a month, for the first quarter, and escalate this amount to $8k in the next quarter, and so on through the year, as their cashflow (and confidence) builds. In the real world, the actual amount of savings they end up with would be the same, but the deposits would look more like this:

1ST QUARTER:	$5k x 3 months =	$ 15k
2ND QUARTER:	$8k x 3 months =	$ 24k
3RD QUARTER:	$12k x 3 months =	$ 36k
4TH QUARTER:	$15k x 3 months =	$ 45k
	Total Profit at year's end =	$120k

This "pay yourself first" approach was typically recommended for the management of personal finances. Thanks to Michalowicz, it's being applied to businesses of all kinds, and is especially effective in law firms to support their profit-building efforts. Since we've introduced the concept to our attorney clients, and encouraged them to read the book, we've seen huge wins. Clients have made a game out of this process and get very excited watching the small, initial deposits in their profit account grow larger throughout the year. We find that once firm owners set up their accounts and commit to this process, they love the idea of proactively building their profit instead of helplessly waiting to see what's left over at the end of the year.

Not surprisingly, they become much more rigorous about which expenses they'll authorize. The commitment to add to their profit account each month puts positive constraints on the firm's spending. So, even though cutting expenses is not the only key to building profitability, it becomes more leveraged when it's done in conjunction with a *Profit First* account. For a more complete look at the details of this approach, we recommend you read the book.

BUDGET

To become more "proactive" in your approach to managing your firm's finances, we recommend you take the guidelines we gave you earlier and create a budget. Some firms have one put together by their CPA or, if they have software that will help them set one up, they can also use their bookkeeper or office manager to create an initial draft. Some use what's called "The Kentucky Windage" approach, which involves using the prior year's numbers and intuitively adding or subtracting a certain percent to each category for the coming year. This semi-scientific approach is not as accurate as we'd like, but it's faster than studying prior years' expenses to establish certain trends – and, if it gets the job done the first year, we're okay with it. Once you have a baseline budget set up, you can continue to refine it in the following years.

Keep in mind that your budget should be done on a cash and accrual basis. Also, be sure to take into account seasonal fluctuations in business to make your budgeting process reflect your firm's historical trends. This will help you anticipate high and low revenue months, as well as time any major cash outlays such as partner distributions and purchases.

If you have partners, your budget is usually discussed at the yearly retreat and then adjusted and adopted. For best results, it should be monitored monthly by the owner or managing partner by looking at your Dashboard, and backed up by your Profit and Loss Statement, to provide additional detail. Your Dashboard will show your revenues, fixed and variable expenses, your client reimbursements, your payroll and your taxes. At the end of the year, you'll have a dozen Dashboards to paint a picture of how your firm performed. From this data, you can look for trends and assess what you need to do to improve cashflow and profits immediately. After a couple of years, you can then track variances from year to year and spot larger trends, such as consistently poor cashflow during certain seasons of the year.

We've attached a Law Firm Budget example at the back of this chapter, but you can find the actual spreadsheet online at:
https://atticusadvantage.com/product/cashflow-profitability/.

RECOVERABLE AND NON-RECOVERABLE EXPENSES

This distinction varies widely from state to state, but generally, copying costs, office supplies and mailing expenses are not recoverable.

Recoverable expenses are those that are passed on to clients, and they're most often seen in litigation practices. The *California Code of Civil Procedure Section 1033.5,* for example, says such costs include court filing fees, law and motion fees, jury fees, expert witness fees (if ordered by the court), service of process, and transcriber expenses associated with depositions. But this list will vary on a state-by-state basis.

EMERGENCY EXPENSES

Finally, because unexpected issues can and will affect your firm, it's critical to have money set aside for emergencies. Catastrophes will happen, whether it's a water main that breaks and floods your office, an electrical storm that fries your computers, or a weather-related disaster that damages your facility. Traditionally, we recommended firms have a plan to cover 90 days of operating expenses to ride out the disaster, but recent circumstances have forever shifted those recommendations.

During the writing of this book, the COVID-19 crisis shut down the economy in much of the world and now qualifies as the single biggest economic disaster the United States – and possibly the world – has ever seen. The extent of this damage is still unclear, but is expected to plunge the economy into a severe recession, if not a depression.

In an attempt to forestall this outcome, the government put together an economic stimulus package consisting of billions of dollars. Even though many firms were able to access funds through the Paycheck Protection Program, Economic Injury Disaster Loans, grants and other SBA programs, the infusion of stimulus money during the crisis required several rounds of authorization by Congress and was fraught with delays and difficulties. Because the loans were dispensed by large banks, firms with established banking relationships tended to get their loans much faster than the smaller firms that needed the money more desperately. Often, small firms lack good banking relationships and tend to operate with limited cash reserves. When they had difficulty accessing government funds in the first round of funding and had to wait months for subsequent rounds, they were devastated by their lack of access to the money they needed to survive.

To cope, many firms created austerity plans that included reducing or withholding shareholder salaries, extensive salary cuts across the board, and eventually laying off or furloughing long-term employees. Needless to say, it was a painful process to witness.

An emergency account capable of covering three months of overhead would have helped, but most solo and small firms lacked even that. Based on how long it will take some firms to recover from this pandemic, we're now recommending you build an account to cover six months of expenses.

Of course, each crisis is different, and whether it's a weather-related disaster or a national health emergency, it's hard to prepare for every eventuality. But there is no question that having ready access to cash gives you options and buys you time.

After 9/11 and the 2008 banking crisis, the two most recent national crises, banks stopped making loans and called for open Lines of Credit to be paid off immediately. Based on that, while the COVID-19 crisis was still in its infancy and banks were not yet pressed into service to disburse stimulus loans, we recommended that firm owners and shareholders immediately open a Line of Credit with their local bank. To avoid a situation in which the bank swept the funds back automatically (this happened in 2008), we then told them to cash it out and put the money in another bank. Many of our clients did this and it helped them bridge the gap as they waited for an agonizing month or two for government funding. Some attorneys even applied for and got Home Equity Lines of Credit out of an abundance of caution.

In any case, this crisis has reinforced two important ideas that will serve you well no matter what kind of crisis you encounter:

- **The importance of building an Emergency Fund.**
  Having several months of operating expenses allowed many firms to go through the initial part of the crisis without panicking and without the need to lay off their team. They were able to go virtual and stayed remarkably productive. Given how long this crisis is lasting, we now believe that up to six months of coverage is preferable.

- **Cultivating a relationship with your bank and the individual lenders who work there.** Firms that received the government loans the fastest were those who had developed good relationships with their bankers. These firms also tended to have their finances very well organized because they'd been through the lending process before. Firms with no banking relationships (whose finances tended to be in disarray), were last in line – even though their need was often greater.

Prepare as best you can for these unexpected events by setting up a separate account that you contribute to over the years. After all, most crises aren't accompanied by huge government stimulus packages, and for you to weather most disasters, you must be self-reliant. We'd prefer that you didn't have to end up relying on credit cards or dipping into a Line of Credit – because you've successfully planned ahead.

When considering where to keep your emergency fund, you'll need to weigh interest rates as well as easy access to funds, to be sure you get the best of both. Estate Planning attorney Victor Medina, an Adjunct Practice Advisor with Atticus and founder of Palante Wealth Advisors, recommends the following options:

1. **High-Yield Bank Accounts.**
   If you can find one with competitive interest rates, no monthly fees or balance requirements, these accounts offer easy access to your money when you need it (and even when you don't, you'll need to resist the urge to dip into these funds for non-emergency needs). Shop around and compare what each bank has to offer. It's a plus if you can find one that awards a "welcome bonus" for opening a new account, but beware that banks are notorious for adding in unexpected fees.

2. **Money Market Accounts.**
   This is another option that offers easy access to your funds, plus a slightly higher rate of return than a checking account –

similar to that of a high-yield savings account. On the down-side, fees for these accounts can eat into your returns, so it's important to shop around for the best deal. Money market accounts are like high-yield savings accounts. Strictly speaking, most money market accounts are forms of mutual funds held at a brokerage firm that pay out a fixed rate of return (higher than both a savings account and CDs). Typically, there are operating costs for the mutual fund, which can range from 0.05% up to 0.5%, depending on the company. You may be limited to transferring a minimum amount out when you want to access it (often requiring transactions of $500 or more). Look at low-cost brokerage houses when weighing options for your money market account.

3. **Certificates of Deposit.**
   Certificates of Deposit (or CDs) are bank instruments that guarantee a specific fixed interest for a term. The longer the term of the CD, the higher the interest rate. This rate will be higher than a savings account, but lower than most everything else. Another downside to using CDs is that you'll incur a penalty if you access your money sooner than the end of the term. That penalty is a clawback of some of the interest credited to the account. One strategy that you can use to mitigate that potential penalty is laddering your CDs so that 20%-25% of that money becomes available every year. Some of that money will still be subject to clawback, but it won't be as bad.

4. **Phantom Partner.**
   One firm we worked with had a novel approach to building up their funds. They were a firm of three equal partners, and, at the end of the year, when taking their distributions, they designated a fourth, or "Phantom Partner," who also received an equal share. Over the years, they found this was a fair and equitable approach to help build up a substantial fund.

Avoid any form of investment or brokerage account with potential variability or risk of loss, recommends Medina. "Your emergency fund should be safe and liquid, so you should avoid stock market investments (stocks, bonds, mutual funds, REITS) – not safe – as well as insurance products (annuities, cash value life insurance) – not liquid." He extends this advice to bonds during this current recovery period, where the selling price of the bond is linked to the current interest rates. Interest rates are currently low, but, if they increase in the future, the value of the bonds will go down. New bonds will be worth more since they'll pay higher interest. That means you'll sell them at a loss if you need to liquidate them quickly (like in an emergency!).

As of this writing, we are in unprecedented territory, but this advice will serve you no matter what crisis you're dealing with in the future. The challenges presented by the COVID-19 pandemic have tested law firms of every size and practice focus. Attorney Medina concludes by saying, "What's important is to learn from the lessons this struggle has provided, and be better positioned for the future. In a crisis, cash-on-hand is king. You owe it to yourself, and your clients, to be in the best cash position possible."

BUSINESS INTERRUPTION INSURANCE

Many firms have business interruption insurance, which is often offered as a rider to their commercial property insurance. These policies can come with a wide range of options that primarily apply to damage of your physical structure. Some policies offer coverage that compensates for lost income during the restoration process only, while others compensate for lost income up to the point that the firm reestablishes its normal level of income. Limitations will vary, but some cover not only lost revenue, but fixed expenses such as rent and utility costs, payroll taxes, and costs associated with establishing a temporary location. As we enter a period where weather patterns are shifting, more and more firms are looking at this kind of coverage as a necessity. Currently, as the effects of the COVID-19 pandemic are unfolding and the impacts on businesses are being evaluated, many businesses plan to claim that the virus was an Act of God similar to a weather disaster. It remains to be seen how the insurance companies will react to this.

Seeking Loans

Keep in mind that if you go to a bank for a loan, under ordinary circumstances, the process will not be quick and you must have your financial house in order. The bank is going to want to see your books. They're not going to gamble on you if you can't produce them and demonstrate that you've got all the proper systems and oversights in place. If you're looking for a large loan, they'll look at your last two years (or more) of quarterly statements and demand a lot of documentation. This can be a painful process, but has motivated more than one of our clients to organize their finances.

The War Chest

For contingency firms that need to fund expensive litigation that may take years to resolve, building a war chest is critical if they don't want to either loan the firm money or seek loans from lenders who charge very steep interest rates. The "Phantom Partner" approach we just described as a way to save for an emergency fund also applies here.

In Conclusion

In this chapter we discussed the fourth element in the **RULES** acronym: **"E"** for **Expenses**, and how they can affect your cashflow and profits. Keep in mind that the percentages we proposed are guidelines, not hard and fast rules you have to match perfectly. As we've mentioned, every firm is different, and there are legitimate exceptions that may make sense to you. Creating and using a budget, a step that many small firms don't take the time for, is critical to plan and control costs, especially when combined with a Monthly Dashboard review. In this chapter, we also introduced you to the *Profit First* approach and encouraged you to establish a separate account to begin building profit as quickly as possible. In the next chapter we'll talk about speed and how it relates to ensuring that your cashflow is positive and your profits are what they should be.

ENDNOTES

1

Results-Oriented Financial Management:
A Step by Step Guide to Law Firm Profitability, John G. Iezzi, CPA
p.48

2

Michalowicz, Mike (2014) Profit First: Transform Your Business from
a Cash-Eating Monster to a Money-Making Machine
p.44

This Law Firm Budget Template may be accessed online at
https://atticusadvantage.com/product/cashflow-profitability/.

		Month 1	Month 2	Month 3
REVENUE				
	Practice Area 1			
	Practice Area 2			
	Service Offering 1			
	Service Offering 2			
	Other Revenue			
	Client Expenses Reimbursed			
	TOTAL REVENUE	$0.00	$0.00	$0.00
OPERATING EXPENSES				
OFFICE				
	Office/Lease			
	Telephone			
	Internet			
	Cell Phone/Data Plan			
	Other Utilities			
	Parking			
	Housekeeping			
	TOTAL OFFICE EXPENSE	$0.00	$0.00	$0.00
INSURANCE				
	Insurance -Professional Liability			
	Insurance -Other			
	TOTAL INSURANCE EXPENSE	$0.00	$0.00	$0.00
LICENSE & PROFESSIONAL FEES & TAXES				
	Business Licence			
	Bar License			
	State Bar Dues			
	Local Bar Dues			
	Other Bar Dues			
	Continuing Legal Education			
	Other Dues			
	Property/Business Taxes			
	TOTAL LICENSE & PROF FEE EXPENSE	$0.00	$0.00	$0.00
TECHNOLOGY/OFFICE				
	Practice Management Software			
	Client Relationship Mgmt Software			
	Online Legal Research			
	Office Suite Software			
	Other Software			
	Office Supplies			
	Courier Services			
	Postage			
	Computer Expense			
	Equipment Rental			
	Equipment Maintenance & Repairs			
	Library Expense			
	TOTAL TECHNOLOGY/OFFICE EXPENSE	$0.00	$0.00	$0.00
PAYROLL EXPENSES/OUTSOURCING				
	Total Salary			
	Payroll Service			
	Independent Contractors			

Virtual Receptionist			
401(k) Administration Fee			
TOTAL PAYROLL EXPENSES	$0.00	$0.00	$0.00
MARKETING/BUSINESS DEVELOPMENT			
Website Hosting			
Advertising			
Inbound Marketing Campaigns			
Conferences/Events			
Client Development Meals			
Travel			
TOTAL MARKETING EXPENSE	$0.00	$0.00	$0.00
BANKING/FINANCES			
Bank Fees			
Finance Charges			
TOTAL BANKING EXPENSE	$0.00	$0.00	$0.00
PROFESSIONAL SERVICES & EXPENSES			
Legal/Accounting Fees			
Digital Marketing/Copywriting			
Graphic Designer			
Business Coaching/Training			
TOT PROFESSIONAL SERV. EXPENSE	$0.00	$0.00	$0.00
OTHER			
Charitable Donations			
Political Contributions			
Emergency Fund			
Profit Account			
TOT CHARITABLE/POLITICAL EXPENSE	$0.00	$0.00	$0.00
CLIENT-RELATED EXPENSES			
Filing Fees			
Court Reporter Fees			
Expert Witness Fees			
Other Fees			
TOTAL CLIENT-RELATED EXPENSES	$0.00	$0.00	$0.00
TOTAL OPERATING EXPENSES	$0.00	$0.00	$0.00
NET PROFIT (PRE-TAX)			
REVENUE-EXPENSES	$0.00	$0.00	$0.00

Chapter 6

SPEED

How The Lack Of Speed Kills Your Profit Margin

"**I**f you bought something three or four months ago and just now got a bill for it, how motivated would you be to pay it?" CPA and long-term Atticus Facilitator, Cammie Hauser, posed this question recently at one of our workshops. She used the question to emphasize the importance of **Speed** as the **"S"** of the **RULES**. Here she was applying it to the time capture, invoicing and collection process. "I'm talking to the hourly billers right now. Because some of you are very slow when it comes to invoicing." A few of the participants with hourly-billing firms looked up. "Unfortunately, time is not your friend when it comes to collecting money. You need to understand that your client's perception of value corrodes over time. When their need is the greatest – usually at the beginning of their case – they value your services highly and are most likely to pay."

She continued, "Unfortunately, as you start to resolve their problem, the urgency associated with their matter starts to drop – and so does their desire to pay. If a month passes, it has dropped even more. The chances of your getting paid, in full, diminish dramatically over time." Cammie brought up a slide illustrating this impact:

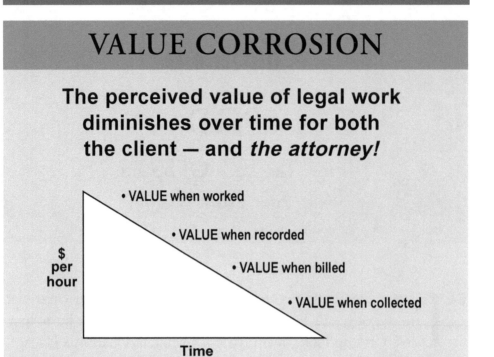

VALUE CORROSION

"The above graphic shows how your hourly rate is effectively diminished over time. Look at the **value when worked** compared to the **value when collected**. There's a huge difference. And here's the worst part: The perceived value of your case diminishes over time for not only the client – but also the attorney. Obviously, clients are less motivated to pay if they're being billed 90 or 120 days after the case is resolved, but it gets worse. Studies show ***the attorney is also less motivated*** to collect for that work! In many cases, they make a feeble attempt or two to collect from clients and then give up – leaving a lot of money on the table."

A client raised his hand and said, "I have an hourly-billing firm. And when new work is coming in, it seems more important than chasing down a client to get him to pay." Cammie agreed. "You're right. That's exactly what happens. Too many attorneys we've worked with have fallen into this trap – prioritizing new work over getting paid.

You have to do both – getting paid is what keeps you in business."

THINK OF IT THIS WAY:
Time not billed is like a free loan to the client.

An Estate Planning attorney piped up and said, "What about fixed-fee practices? We usually get paid upfront, or at least by the document delivery meeting. We don't really have collection problems." Cammie replied, "You're right. So, for your practice, the focus on speed shifts. In fixed-fee practices, what matters is keeping track of Time On Desk and working to reduce that time. The faster you can complete the work in a fixed-fee matter – without sacrificing quality – the more profitable that matter will be and the more you can do in a year."

She then turned to a group of family law attorneys gathered at a table. "Now, some of you family law attorneys who handle complex divorces with high-net-worth clients prefer to bill on an hourly basis. And that's okay – you're dealing with cases that are especially difficult to predict. Some of you even handle celebrity clients and famous athletes. On *Cobb's Value Curve* that we discussed earlier, they land in the zone where results are more important to the client than the fees. You just want to avoid collection problems by getting a large retainer upfront and getting a new retainer prior to going to trial."[1]

She then turned to the PI attorneys in the room. "In PI firms, there's yet another focus on speed: For you, it's important to reduce the amount of time it takes to collect from insurance companies. We're going to talk about that in a moment." (If you're a PI attorney, skip the credit card discussion and go to the section entitled *Speed and Litigation Firms.*)

CREDIT CARDS

For those firms that must bill their clients on an hourly basis, there are ways to speed up the process. The American Bar Association has permitted law firms to accept credit card payments since 1974, but a surprising number of firms have been slow to make the switch. While there are ethical considerations to ponder before adopting this option, it's well worth the time and energy to find the proper fit. According to *Clio's 2019 Legal Trends Report*, law firms that accept credit cards are paid almost 40% more quickly. Given everything we know about how value corrodes over time, this should be a no-brainer for most firms.[2]

Consumers are accustomed to the convenience of making payments with credit cards; they like the ease of it and the possibility of accumulating points. As a result, accepting credit card payments not only increases client satisfaction, it also improves law firm collection rates. A win-win all around.

Some firms have added a clause to their fee agreement that authorizes the firm to use the client's credit card if they don't receive payment of an invoice 10 days after it is sent. To do this, the firm must have the ability to safeguard that client's credit card information. Those who aren't comfortable with this will let clients use their cards in the office. Any number of card readers may be used for this process, and card companies usually offer several options.

If you've decided to take the plunge and accept credit card payments, or if you're interested in upgrading your current card company, look for the following features and benefits:

Next Day Funding

Ideally, your credit card company would provide rapid funding within 12 hours. This is what's commonly referred to as "next day" funding. You may not get this service for free, but, even with a small fee, it's worth it.

IOLTA Compliance

In order to comply with IOLTA, make sure that your credit card company guarantees that no processing fees will be withdrawn from your trust account. Since not all card companies are the same, and the rules vary from state to state, you must take care to check on this. There are several ways to resolve this issue that offer different levels of compliance, so work with the card company to avoid running afoul of the rules. Again, keep in mind that the rules and requirements for trust accounts vary by state, so check with your local Bar if you have any questions about how your merchant account is to be handled.

Refund Rules

Many credit card companies restrict payment for "refundable" items, and this can pose a major problem. If you take a credit card payment for what Rule 3-700(D)(2) of the *Rules of Professional Conduct* defines as a "True Retainer" (also known as a "Classic Retainer"), your retainer is meant "to secure an attorney's availability over a given period of time. Thus, such a fee is earned by the attorney when paid since the attorney is entitled to the money regardless of whether he actually performs any services for the client." A True Retainer reserves the attorney's time and is "considered ***earned upon receipt*** because it takes the attorney out of the marketplace and precludes him from taking other legal work."[3]

This type of retainer is rare these days and must be spelled out to the client. Retainers that are not considered "True" or "Classic" are often characterized as more of an "Advance Payment" option and are typically applied to future work. They are considered **refundable** when that work, or a portion of that work, is not done.

So, in order to be in compliance with trust accounting rules and those of the card company, be sure you understand what kind of retainer you're being paid before you accept payment by credit card.

SOFTWARE INTEGRATION

Ask if the payment processing company can integrate with your time and billing software for seamless processing. This reduces the time invested in the billing process for you and your team.

MONTHLY OR QUARTERLY PAYMENT PLANS

In practice areas where the fees are significant, see if the card company can provide a payment plan with an "auto-billing" feature to bill your clients for a specific amount of money every month.

FINANCING OPTIONS

If you're interested in a credit card that will help you finance firm expenses, look for one that offers an interest-free financing period. Offers change frequently, but, as of this writing, some credit card companies offer a 0% APR introductory financing on new purchases for up to 12 months. Be sure to read the fine print to see what happens once the 12 months are up.

FEE CLASSIFICATIONS

Not all payments by credit card are classified the same way. Currently, Visa and Mastercard have different classifications for payments made in person, over the phone and online. Be sure you understand these differences to gain the most flexibility.

KNOW YOUR REAL RATE

Currently, there are at least 600 credit card fee categories, and which ones apply to you is a closely guarded secret. In the past 10 years, hidden credit card fees have escalated and, because of this, a low initial base rate of 2% can easily become an effective rate of 3% or more.

This is because credit card companies have found a way to monetize nearly every activity associated with them. Typical credit card fees include, but are not limited to:

- an additional card fee
- an annual fee
- a balance transfer fee
- a cash advance fee
- a credit limit increase fee
- an expedited payment fee
- an express card delivery fee
- a foreign transaction fee
- a late fee
- an over limit fee
- a paper statement or copying fee
- a returned payment fee
- a reward recovery or reinstatement fee
- a reward redemption fee
- set-up fees
- maintenance fees

So do your homework. Ask questions and read the small print to ensure your rates remain as advertised over time. Some of our attorney clients have raised their rates 5% or 10% across the board to compensate, in part, for these fees. Whether you raise your fees slightly or absorb the costs, accepting payment by credit cards is still better than chasing clients for payment. In the end, the fact that you've shifted the collection problem to the credit card company, and you get paid 40% faster, makes the hassle worthwhile.

TIME AND BILLING SOFTWARE

If you have an hourly-billing firm, using time and billing software is a very effective way of making sure your team doesn't lose credit for any work they've done. As of this writing, some software systems track everything your employee does in programs like Microsoft Word and Microsoft Outlook and attaches it to the appropriate file automatically. Such time-tracking software can be more accurate than even the most fastidious employee, and, because it tracks every hour, you'll see an immediate increase in your cashflow. And higher cashflow is going to lead to more profitability. Check the *Capterra website (www.capterra.com)* for the most up-to-date reviews on this kind of software.

LEGAL BILLING SOFTWARE

But that's not the only way technology can help you. With the right software, law firms can bill electronically and avoid the time-consuming, paper-intensive and costly process of creating, printing and mailing invoices. Currently, there are two choices when it comes to electronic billing: You can use the billing features built into practice management software, or use a stand-alone software system that integrates with your accounting tools.

As of this writing, practice management software companies like Clio, Rocket Matter, Mycase and others, offer the ability to generate invoices from time entries by using built-in time tracking tools. Some providers also include trust accounting reconciliation features and options to integrate your firm's general accounting information into your billing system. Since each system offers a unique mix of features and benefits, we recommend you examine each of their offerings, pick your top two or three, then rigorously test the invoicing tools during your free trial period. You want a system that maximizes convenience and streamlines the whole process. And for the sake of the client, you want the software to generate invoices that are:

1. **Customizable:** The look of your invoices should be consistent with your firm's letterhead and logo.

2. **Easy to edit:** You want to retain the ability to make

changes. Remember to include action words in your description of the work.

3. **Easy to read:** Make sure the finished invoice has a font that is large and understandable.

4. **Easy to share with your clients:** The final product should be shareable by e-mail, text and PDF, if needed.

Taking it a step further, several software systems currently offer the option of including a payment link in their invoices that allows clients to go to a payment page that accepts their credit card. This new interface doesn't require clients to create a password or log in. This eliminates several steps and encourages a faster response from the client, who can pay online from their computer, cell phone or tablet. In this system, which is different from a payment portal, the client enters their credit card information, but the firm never has possession of the information. When the firm does not have to encrypt and store credit card information, its liability is dramatically reduced.

ONLINE PAYMENTS ARE INCREASINGLY POPULAR

Since the ease and convenience of online payment options is so appealing to clients, many large and mid-sized firms put online payment portals on their website. Unlike the payment page just described, portals offer a "payment gateway" that encrypts sensitive credit card details and allows the firm to accept online payments promptly and securely. Portals are typically password protected but, overall, this process still saves your client's time when compared to writing checks and licking stamps. According to Jeff Shavitz, founder of LexCharge, "The good news for solo and small-firm lawyers who accept online payments via credit card, ACH or eChecks is that doing so increases client satisfaction and allows your law firm to compete with the whopping 62% of large and mid-sized firms that are already offering these options to their clients." [4]

BITCOIN AND BLOCKCHAIN

The 2019 ABA Tech Show, which featured a panel entitled "Bitcoin and Blockchain for Lawyers," projected that more firms will accept cryptocurrency as payment for their services in the near future. Despite the volatility and uncertainty associated with digital currency today, it's expected to surge in popularity in the years to come. And who knows? A few leading-edge, large firms have already adopted this form of payment, but currently it's unclear when it will be legitimized enough to be accepted across the board.

SPEED AND LITIGATION FIRMS

Now let's look at the concept of speed when it's applied to contingency firms, such as Plaintiff's Personal Injury firms. Things are different here. While it's important to track Time On Desk to be sure cases are continually progressing and being closed out in a timely manner, Atticus Practice Advisor Patrick Wilson advises a "Quick, Slow, Quick" approach. He believes new cases should get worked up quickly, allowed to move slowly as treatment proceeds, and then get resolved quickly at the end. This means most of the attorney's labor is applied at the beginning and end of the process, though they, or their team, stay in touch with the client and monitor the case as it progresses.

In all cases, the average fee of each case should be maximized and not sacrificed for the sake of speed. This is especially important with severe injury cases in which clients will take time to reach maximum medical improvement, and complex cases that require special expertise and time to develop. Not speeding these cases to conclusion can positively impact the value of the case and the outcome for the client.

But there's another area in which speed is important: Shortening the time it takes to be paid by insurance companies. Since insurance companies generate a large part of their revenue by investing the dollars their policyholders pay for premiums, the longer this money sits in their investment accounts the more interest it accumulates. It's in their best interest to delay payouts for as long as possible to secure the maximum interest possible. Of course, that's not their only strategy: In direct opposition to the caring message communicated by their ads, they'll also work hard to minimize the value of the policyholder's claims. Some states specify how long insurance companies have to provide settlement funds after receiving a signed release form, and some do not. In the states that do, insurance companies still find ways to delay releasing the funds. They may, for example, get the release form but take a while entering it into their system, delaying the point at which the countdown begins for them to release the funds. This is just one example of the extreme stalling strategies they may pursue.

Unwittingly, many attorneys add to the length of time it takes to collect settlements by shifting their attention to new cases and not properly tracking maturing cases. Aware of this shift in attention, and how this lack of attention delays payment, some firms resolve this issue by:

1. Only issuing attorney bonuses after the firm has received the funds and never before. This means the attorney will continue to pay attention to the case instead of turning all of their attention to new cases.

2. Pro-rating the time to collect the settlement (six weeks is typical), and reducing the attorney's bonus by how long it takes the firm to be paid. In other words, the attorney is paid less the longer it takes the firm to be paid. This serves to incentivize the attorney to stay in the game.

HIRE A SETTLEMENT COORDINATOR

Many firms – typically large and mid-sized ones – deal with this issue by hiring a Settlement Coordinator to manage and speed up this process. A Settlement Coordinator in a PI firm is responsible for managing the settlement phase for all their assigned cases. Typically, once the attorney or case manager confirms that a client has completed treatment with their medical provider, they're introduced to the Settlement Coordinator, who becomes the client's main contact person until the funds are dispersed.

The Coordinator is responsible for negotiating reductions from medical providers, ensuring medical providers are properly paid, and ensuring the final settlement check is paid to the client. Different firms will utilize their Settlement Coordinator in different ways, but the list below shows how one firm does it. According to their website, the Zane Law Group describes the responsibilities of their Settlement Coordinator as follows:

1. Contact clients every two weeks to stay updated about their condition.

2. Respond quickly to client communications and any new case developments.

3. Maintain medical records and create a billing inventory, staying in touch with medical providers to be sure the client's case is current.

4. Ensure clients receive the maximum benefits by understanding the health insurance billing processes.

5. Update the client's information with regard to advances, health insurance liens, provider liens and super liens.

6. Coordinate the signing of release documents with insurance adjusters, defense counsel and clients.

7. Handle Medicare claims and move them to conclusion.

8. Verify that AHCCS, Medicare and ERISA chronologies are up-to-date.

9. Work to obtain reductions from AHCCS, hospitals and any other party owed compensation for working on the client's case.

10. Generate all documentation relative to the processing of a client's case, in addition to preparing the settlement packets.

11. Coordinate with the firm's accounting person to deposit the insurance checks in the trust account and issue checks to lien holders, the clients and the firm.

Candidates for this position must possess a high level of accuracy and detail-orientation, a thorough understanding of legal documents and processes in Personal Injury firms, plus a strong affinity for numbers and accounting-type functions.

They must also have excellent communication skills and several years of experience working in a Personal Injury law firm. If a firm can find the right candidate, he or she can speed up the release of funds and make an enormous difference in the cashflow and profitability of the firm.

In Conclusion

In this chapter we discussed the final element in the **RULES** acronym: **"S"** for **Speed.** We've seen that the proper application of speed can make a huge difference in a firm's cashflow and profitability, but is so often neglected. We also discussed how increasing speed means different things in different practice areas. For hourly-billing practices, the emphasis is on reducing the amount of time from when the work is done to when it's billed and finally collected. For flat-fee firms, the emphasis is on speeding the work through the firm's Work In Progress to reduce every file's Time On Desk. And for many contingency firms, the focus shifts to collecting from institutions more quickly – especially those who will delay paying as long as possible. Hopefully, we've given you enough examples to demonstrate where you can put the pedal to the metal in your firm.

ENDNOTES

1

William C. Cobb of Cobb Consulting,
www.cobb-consulting.com

2

Clio's 2019 Legal Trends Report,
www.clio.com/legal-trends/2019-report

3

Majlaw.com/non-refundable-retainer-provisions-in-fee-agreements-
are-they-proper/Michael Fish

4

American Bar Association, October 2018, Does Your Law Firm
Accept Only Cash and Checks? You're Losing Money, americanbar.
org/news/abanews/publications/youraba/2018/does-your-law-firm-
accept-only-cash-and-checks—you're-losing-mon/

FINAL WORDS

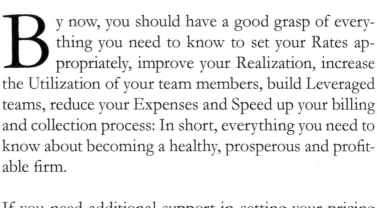

By now, you should have a good grasp of everything you need to know to set your Rates appropriately, improve your Realization, increase the Utilization of your team members, build Leveraged teams, reduce your Expenses and Speed up your billing and collection process: In short, everything you need to know about becoming a healthy, prosperous and profitable firm.

If you need additional support in setting your pricing structure, reducing your collections, structuring performance-based compensation plans, building a more motivated and profitable team, or dealing with any issue concerning your firm finances, let us know. We work with individual attorneys and firms all over the United States and Canada to help them reach the financial goals they thought were out of their reach. In addition, we help partnerships that are dealing with pending retirement issues, personality conflicts, possible mergers and re-organization issues. We have customized retreats, one-on-one business coaching and many group programs to fit your particular needs.

For full-sized downloads of the forms featured in this book, plus additional resources, go to:
https://atticusadvantage.com/product/cashflow-profitability/.

APPENDIX #1

Proactive Strategy Four: Select Clients Wisely

In our effort to give you the strategies and tools to improve your time management, we want to bring to your attention that even the subtlest behaviors can sabotage your goal. You may be asking yourself, "How does the way I select my clients affect how much time I have to get my work done?" This chapter will answer that question and give you a system for client selection. We also identify ways that clients can be a drain on your time and eventually your well-being and, on the other hand, how they can be an asset to your practice.

Why Be So Selective?

If we were to apply Pareto's Principle, also known as the 80/20 Rule, to your client base, we would probably find that 80% of your income comes from 20% of your clients. Hidden among the clients that you serve, they are a small, quiet, but vitally important group. Studies show that this 20% of your clients who provide the most income have certain characteristics. If you can learn to recognize those characteristics, you can begin to target them as future clients and raise the percentage of your more profitable clients.

Before we introduce our system for selecting clients, we would like to touch on some of the factors that make it crucial for you to implement some plan for selectivity.

How to Tell the "Good" Clients From the "Bad"

The client selection task that faces attorneys is more difficult than that of many professionals due to the volatile nature of many clients and their disputes. Nice, normally well-grounded and cooperative individuals can engage in uncharacteristically extreme behavior during the course of your representation. It can be very difficult to tell the good clients from the bad when they are on an emotional roller-coaster.

Given the emotional state of many clients, you must be particularly selective, as this extreme behavior can negatively impact you and your staff through large amounts of time lost and scheduled time being disrupted. Below are some examples of "bad" clients:

- Clients who are excessively needy and compelled to talk about their situation endlessly to attorneys and/or staff members
- Clients who refuse to take responsibility for their actions and any contribution they may have made to the current breakdown, problem or dispute
- Clients who are deceptive in an attempt to protect themselves and their interests
- Clients who withhold information or stall in complying with your requests due to mistrust
- Clients who are so consumed with their dilemma that they cannot focus on or follow through with your instructions

Unless you practice "threshold law" (you take anybody who crosses your threshold), you likely have developed a means of identifying "good" clients. We have taken what you instinctively know about client selection and developed selection criteria to make the process easier and a little more scientific. This selection process centers on what we call the **client scorecard**—a form that enables you to rank clients in certain critical categories. By making the process quantifiable, you can now have members of your staff pre-interview and rate prospective clients on the phone. Especially if your initial consultations are free, this will eliminate your having to spend many unproductive hours interviewing what may turn out to be a "bad" client.

Case Study
Time Management Issue: Coaching Prospects Saves Time

Attorney: Harriett Steinberg
State: New York

After many years of practice, Harriett has developed great sensitivity to the timing issues inherent in the client selection process. When a marriage begins to deteriorate, a certain amount of time is required for both parties to work through the phases of shock, anger, and acceptance that accompany the process. Even for the initiating spouse, divorce is a lengthy process that shouldn't be undertaken prematurely. Harriett has gained the wisdom to recognize that if you sign clients up too early, you spin your wheels, spend their money needlessly, and don't satisfy them, because they weren't really ready to move forward. She now operates as a sort of coach with clients who come to her too early in the process. She encourages these clients to take stock and to consider other actions before hiring her and filing for divorce. Experience has shown it's a waste of her time to begin the process prematurely—even when the clients don't recognize this fact themselves.

Harriett's Good Advice:
Don't spin your wheels. Have the sensitivity to recognize where clients are in terms of readiness and give them recommendations that will support them. Having done this, you are guaranteed to see them return when they're ready.

Adopting the Client Scorecard Method of Selection

As you read through this discussion, look at the client scorecard that follows as Example 4-1. The categories on the scorecard are those we deem the most critical when it comes to selecting clients:

- Cooperation and credibility
- Ability to pay
- Case value
- Type of work (is it the type of work you prefer?)
- Referral source

Our ranking system is based on four levels: A, B, C and D clients. The A clients score the highest in each category; D clients score the lowest.

You can modify the form to suit your own needs. For example, some attorneys may assign a different weight to each category. Many of the attorneys we work with weigh the *ability to pay* pretty heavily. For these attorneys, a client who scores an A in every category but cannot pay for services is immediately downgraded to a D level.

For other attorneys, the *opposing counsel* category can be a deal-killer. Their experiences with some opposing counsel have been so negative that even if a client is a high scorer in every category but this one, they refuse to take the case. Alternatively, some of our clients simply raise the cost to the client based on what they fondly call the "jerk premium." They know that the extra work generated by the opposing attorney's tactics warrants the higher fee and openly discuss this with the potential client.

For an example of how a specific type of practice would customize a scorecard, here are the criteria used in a family law practice:

- Availability of assets
- Client personality and credibility
- Level of income
- Attitude toward children
- Case complexity
- Level of spousal animosity
- Opposing counsel
- Referral source

Read through our example of a client selection scorecard and use it as is, or modify it to suit your particular practice. Think about the clients you consider to be "A" level and those who have been "D" level. Add your own criteria to the scorecard to ensure that it reflects the issues you must consider before working with a client.

EXAMPLE 4-1: A, B, C, AND D CLIENT SELECTION SCORECARD

Rank	Client Personality	Type of Work	Case Value	Ability to Pay	Referral Source
A	Cooperative	Most Preferred Work	High Fees	No Problem	Sends Very Good Work
B	Cooperative	Semi-preferred Work	Medium Fees	Slight Problem	Medium-Level Source
C	High Maintenance, Not Cooperative	Not Preferred Work	Low Fees	Low or Slow to Pay	Referred by C-Level Source
D	High Maintenance, Very Difficult	Work Outside Your Expertise	Low or No Fees	Very Low or No Ability to Pay	Referred by D-Level Source

Putting the Client Scorecard into Practice

With this form you can now score potential clients and make a logical decision whether or not to take them. You can do this during

> ### "It is better to *not* do the work and not get paid rather than *do* the work and not get paid."
> ### —Jay Foonberg

or right after your first client interview, but you risk wasting time when there is a better way. We suggest that you create a system around this form that allows you to score the clients on the phone *prior* to their first visit and then, if they appear to be qualified, continue the scoring process when they come in. Remember, however, that it is not usually the best use of your time to screen potential clients on the phone. That is best left to staff who have been trained on how to use the client scorecard. The best situation is to have a designated **intake person** who is on the alert for desirable levels of clients and has a keen sense for financial- and personality-based red flags.

What makes many clients "the wrong kind" is their habit of not paying for services rendered. Your accounts receivable report might indicate that you have not been the best at judging a client's ability to pay in the past. The questions that follow are very important, as the answers will suggest the degree of a potential client's financial stability. Any that indicate instability should be seen as "red flags."

- Did the client find you through print media or online?
- Was the client referred by a local Bar referral service?
- Was the client referred by a C or D client?
- Is the client's first question "How much is this going to cost me?"
- Does the client mention that he/she knows another lawyer who is cheaper?
- Does the client resist paying a consultation fee or a retainer or only pay half?
- Does the client hold out the promise of other work in order to get a discount?
- Does the client mention that he/she is switching attorneys or has switched attorneys midstream?
- Is the client a distant family member with a large matter?

It is possible to have a plan to filter out prospective nonpaying clients. If any of your clients exhibit these warning signs, think twice about working with them.

Aside from financial risk, there might be personality-based warning signs that could indicate future problems. Pay attention to these signs before you admit these troublesome clients into your practice. Level C and D clients do not sneak into your practice unannounced. They usually arrive at your door waving several red flags and you let them in—usually because you need the money, and because you are hoping that the uneasy feeling you felt upon meeting them was just heartburn. Begin to trust that uneasy feeling. It might be trying to tell you that you are getting involved with the wrong kind of client.

- Did the new client show up with a full-blown crisis and demand your full and immediate attention right from the start?
- Did the client display a level of anger totally out of proportion to the matter?
- Is the client seeking revenge or does he/she have some other hidden agenda?
- Does the client want you to guarantee a particular outcome?
- Can the litigation client hear an objective, realistic appraisal of his/her case?
- Does the client have a bad attitude toward lawyers?
- Does the client act displeased no matter how well you take care of him or her?
- Does the client refuse to take responsibility for his or her own actions?
- Did the client arrive late to the first meeting and neglect to bring documents that you requested?

Case Study
Time Management Issue: Spotting Troublesome Clients

Attorney: Caroline Black
State: Florida

A prospective client came in for an initial consultation with attorney Caroline Black several years ago. She was a nice, well-dressed, professional-looking and attractive person. Caroline describes her as having an innocent, "puppy dog" face. Caroline began working with her in good faith and discovered her client was extremely manipulative, always pulling strings, and distorting the truth to serve herself. Over the next three years, the client racked up $50,000 in unpaid attorney's fees and began forging her husband's name on checks. Willing to give her a chance, Caroline tried every reasonable means of working with her, but finally had to cease representation due to the financial damage and emotional strain. Not surprisingly, this client went on to work with *six* more attorneys, all who no doubt believed her to be credible—at least at the beginning.

Caroline's Good Advice:
Get out as soon as possible when you discover that clients are manipulative, can't be trusted, and don't pay for your services. Don't continue to believe what clients say when it is not consistent with what they do. Have an **exit clause in your retainer** so that you are covered in case you need to pull out.

Atticus Tip:
When prospective clients mention that they have worked with one or more previous attorneys on the case they bring to you, it is a warning sign. Very often the other attorneys haven't been paid or were paid a small, initial retainer to begin work. Always ask this question in the very beginning of your interactions with prospective clients: "Have you retained any other attorneys on this matter in the past?" If the answer is yes, proceed with caution. Before taking the client, call the other attorney(s) to learn the status of the case and listen for comments on your prospective client's behavior. This simple step might save you a great deal of trouble.

Suggested Scripts for Client Intake

When your staff person is conducting a client intake interview, he or she should ask questions that point to problem areas. It is helpful to have scripts for him or her to follow. The script provides consistency and thoroughness, and can serve as a training aid. Here are some ideas for scripts:

EXAMPLE 4-2: NEW CLIENT INTAKE SCRIPT (INITIAL)

Caller: "I'd like to talk to an attorney."

Receptionist: "I am going to put you through to _____. She can help you set up an appointment and also answer any questions you might have."

Intake person: (The intake person should have the new client scorecard in hand to evaluate the caller for this exchange.) "Hello, this is _____ and I can help you set up an appointment. But first, whom may we thank for sending you to our office?"

Caller: (Potential "red flag" answers)
- "I found you on the internet."
- "The referral service at the Bar sent me."
- "My friend, (names a C or D client), sent me."

(Preferred answers)
- "You were highly recommended by (names a good referral source)."
- "My friend, (names an A or B client)."

The *red flag answers* tell you to proceed with caution. You may wish to move gracefully into mentioning the consultation fee, because clients who come from the red-flag sources named above will most likely be very price-sensitive, with the possible exception of the caller referred by your past client. When they hear the fee for the initial consultation, they may realize they've called the wrong law office, saving you from a client who won't pay. You may want to give them the names of some other attorneys who don't charge for their initial consultations. The tone of the conversation should always be friendly and helpful, not condescending, when turning away a client.

The *preferred answers* are the first indication that this may be a very good client and you should proceed with the conversation. Some lawyers prefer that the consultation fee be mentioned here. Alternatively, some mention fees after they go through a subsequent fact-finding conversation.

The next part of the pre-screening intake script requires a helpful, gently inquiring tone and shouldn't be rushed, as the intake person is inquiring about very personal issues. Not all attorneys are comfortable having their staff take it to the next level of questioning. This must be undertaken by someone with experience in dealing with clients, who is sensitive to their situation yet knows how to gracefully ask for enough information to qualify them. A long-time paralegal who has been acting as a "designated hitter" in your practice, or an associate who has experience with clients, qualifies. We discuss the term *designated hitter* in more detail in the next chapter of this book. For now, think of the designated hitter as someone who is trained to shoulder many of the lower-level communication tasks for the attorney.

The initial intake and the appointment pre-qualification are the first level of ranking using the scorecard. All the information gathered by the intake person is preliminary. However, it should be adequate to determine either that an appointment is warranted (because the client looks like an A or B client) or that referral to another attorney is more appropriate.

You will gather much more detail in the actual initial consultation with the client. It is helpful to go into the consultation armed with the facts, prepared for the client, advance information in hand, and ready to make a good impression. Clients who have been pre-screened have a much higher conversion rate than non-screened clients.

One of the most important skills for an attorney is the ability to attract clients. Without clients coming through the door on a regular basis, your law practice will not survive. Unfortunately, all clients are not created equal. The clients who tell you they came to you through a low-ranking referral source are not quite the same as those sent to you by your best referral source.

How to Make the Transition to a Practice with Only Good Clients

If you find that you have stocked your practice with C- and D-level clients, it is time to conduct a housecleaning. Many attorneys are appalled to discover just how many problematic clients they have, but there is a solution. A lawyer who recently attended one of our seminars was so taken with the idea of finding out how many problematic clients he had that he went home and spent most of the night ranking his clients. As he suspected, the reason he was becoming so disillusioned with his practice was due to the fact that 80% of his caseload was made up of C- and D-level clients.

To conduct your own housecleaning, choose a time after hours when you are alone in the office, or make it a group effort and go through the client list with your staff. Staff, by the way, usually have an unerring sense of who the A- and B-level clients are. They take the abuse that sometimes comes from C and D clients and know exactly who the more vocal or demanding ones are.

Take a Quick Look at Your Caseload

Before you begin, you can get some idea whether you have an overload of problematic clients by completing Exercise 4-1.

EXERCISE 4-1: SYMPTOMS OF A PRACTICE WITH MANY C- AND D-LEVEL CLIENTS

Instructions: Read through the following checklist. Place a check beside the situations that occur in your practice.

❏ High outstanding receivables—doing quite a bit of work for which you or your team will not be paid.

❏ Clients leave prematurely or often threaten to seek the services of another attorney.

❏ Clients fail to show for scheduled appointments.

❏ Clients fail to bring requested documents or to follow direction.

❏ Staff feel abused by clients who misdirect their anger and scream at them or act unreasonably.

❏ There is a constant sense of crisis and tension that is attributable to specific clients and/or specific opposing counsel.

❏ Staff and attorneys dread going to work and dealing with certain clients.

❏ Staff and attorneys are conscious of not meeting the high expectations of some clients.

❏ Staff and attorneys never hear "thank you" or any acknowledgment for their efforts—even when major victories occur.

Clean Up Your Caseload

If, according to Exercise 4-1, you have a practice with many C and D clients, you may be thinking about *how* to clean up your caseload. We encourage you to read through and take the steps listed here. You'll be surprised at how energizing it is to take control of your practice in this way.

- **Step One:** Go through your case list and rank your current clients A, B, C or D. Note the A and B clients, which you'll keep, and identify the C and D clients.

- **Step Two:** If you think any of your borderline C clients can be "rehabilitated" and upgraded to a B level, sit down and have a very straight conversation with them about what they are doing that is a problem (need to bring payments current, need to start producing documentation that is required, need to stop canceling meetings, etc.). Some will respond positively to this approach; some will not. Take the rest of your C clients and refer them to another attorney if their issues are *personality-based*, not *payment-based*. Avoid sending clients who won't pay to another attorney.

- **Step Three:** Let your D clients go. Write them a letter, let them know in person, or phone them. Check your local rules to be sure you follow the proper protocol. If you decide to write a letter, your Bar association likely has sample disengagement letters that you can adapt. In this chapter, we have also included sample forms and letters for your reference as Examples 4-3, 4-4, 4-5, 4-6, 4-7, and 4-8. If you decide to decline representation after research or investigation, you should protect yourself and your client by (1) promptly advising the client in writing of your decision not to take the case or matter; (2) informing the client of his or her right to contact another lawyer for a second opinion; and (3) informing the client that his or her prompt attention is required. Disengagement and non-engagement letters are especially critical when a lawyer decides not to continue past a specific stage in a case.

If you decide to let the client go in a face-to-face exchange, you need to have a plan. Refer to the guidelines in Exercise 4-2, How to Fire Clients Face to Face, to help you prepare.

EXERCISE 4-2: HOW TO FIRE CLIENTS FACE TO FACE

Instructions: Follow your local rules regarding releasing a client, especially if you are currently in litigation. (Your local rules supersede any advice given here.) Consider having a paralegal or legal assistant in the meeting if you really feel the client may react irrationally and later accuse you of misconduct. Under normal circumstances you won't have to take this extra precaution, but don't fail to document this meeting by summarizing the discussion in a letter and sending a copy to the client by certified mail. Put a copy in your own file to protect yourself in case of a complaint.

Follow these steps:

1. Try to set the client up for the firing conversation and limit his or her reaction by saying, "You may not like what I am going to tell you, but. . . ."

2. Give the client the context for your decision so they will not think it is completely arbitrary. Link your decision to their attitudes and/or behaviors. Give specific examples of where the communication broke down, where they were uncooperative, where they were rude or abusive to you or your staff, or where they failed to pay.

3. Explain why the behaviors and/or attitudes expressed by the client make it uncomfortable, unethical or inappropriate for you to continue representation. Be factual and objective.

4. Give the client an opportunity to respond, ask questions or express anger. Resist being pulled into a discussion that escalates into a fight. Defensiveness only intensifies emotions. Stay in control of the conversation by managing your own emotions.

5. If appropriate, act as a helpful resource and make recommendations as to how the client should proceed. You may recommend counseling or a legal service agency, or offer the names of other attorneys who may help. (Remember to be very careful when referring unstable personalities and non-paying clients to your colleagues.) Call and discuss the situation beforehand to be certain the attorney wants to take this person on.

EXAMPLE 4-3: SAMPLE NON-ENGAGEMENT LETTER

DATE

NAME
ADDRESS
CITY, STATE & ZIP

RE: [SUBJECT]

Dear:

You have contacted this firm and requested that I evaluate whether the firm will represent you in the above-referenced matter. I met with you on [*date*], and have also reviewed the various copies of documents you left with me. I herewith return those documents for your use.

I appreciate the confidence you have expressed in our firm, but, for various reasons, the firm has decided not to represent you in this matter. However, if you have a need in the future for legal assistance, I hope you will again consider our firm.

You should be aware that the passage of time might bar you from pursuing whatever, if any, claim you have in this matter. Accordingly, because time is always important and could be critically short in your case, I recommend you immediately contact another firm for assistance.

In declining to undertake this matter, the firm is not expressing an opinion on whether you might prevail if the action is pursued. You should not refrain from seeking legal assistance from another firm because of any interpretation you may place on this firm's decision not to go forward with this matter.

In accordance with our standard policy, we are not charging you for any legal fees or expenses. While we do charge for evaluating cases, that is only when we express an opinion on the merits of the matter to the client. Since we are not expressing an opinion in this instance, no charge is being made.

Although I believe this letter fully covers all pertinent matters, please call me if you have any questions.

Sincerely,

[*signature*]

Reference: LOMAS, The Florida Bar, *Administrative Forms Handbook.*
Reprinted with permission.

EXAMPLE 4-4: SAMPLE NON-ENGAGEMENT LETTER

(*May be sent by certified mail, with a return receipt requested*)

DATE

NAME
ADDRESS
CITY, STATE & ZIP

RE: [SUBJECT]

Dear:

The purpose of this letter is to confirm, based on our conversation of [*date*], that [*insert firm name*] has decided not to represent you because [*insert reason for declination; if possible and appropriate, state it*]. Our decision to decline this case should not be construed as a statement of the merits of your case.

You should be aware that any action in this matter must be filed within the applicable statute of limitations. I strongly recommend that you consult with another lawyer concerning your rights in this matter.

Very truly yours,

[*signature*]

Reference: LOMAS, The Florida Bar, *Administrative Forms Handbook*.
Reprinted with permission.

EXAMPLE 4-5: SAMPLE NON-ENGAGEMENT LETTER AFTER REVIEW

DATE

NAME
ADDRESS
CITY, STATE & ZIP

RE: [SUBJECT]

Dear:

You have contacted this firm and requested that I evaluate whether the firm will represent you in a claim you believe should be filed against [*insert appropriate name(s)*]. I met with you yesterday and have reviewed various documents you left with me. I enclose those documents for your file.

I appreciate the confidence you have expressed in our firm, but, for various reasons, the firm has decided not to represent you in this matter. However, if you have a need in the future for legal assistance, I hope you will again consider our firm.

You should be aware that the passage of time may bar you from pursuing whatever, if any, claim you may have against [*insert appropriate name(s)*]. Because time is always important and could be critically short in your case, I recommend you immediately contact another firm for assistance.

In declining to undertake this matter, the firm is not expressing an opinion on whether you will prevail if a complaint is filed. You should not refrain from seeking legal assistance from another firm because of any interpretation you may place on this firm's decision not to go forward with this matter.

In accordance with our standard policy, we are not charging you for any legal fees or expenses. While we do charge for evaluating cases, that is only when we express an opinion on the merits of the case to the client. Since we are not expressing an opinion in this instance, no charge is being made.

Although I believe this letter fully covers all pertinent matters, please call me if you have any questions.

Very truly yours,

[*signature*]

Reference: LOMAS, The Florida Bar, *Administrative Forms Handbook.*
Reprinted with permission.

EXAMPLE 4-6: SAMPLE NON-ENGAGEMENT LETTER— DECLINING CASE AFTER RESEARCH OR INVESTIGATION

DATE

NAME
ADDRESS
CITY, STATE & ZIP

RE: [SUBJECT]

Dear:

Pursuant to my letter of [*date*], we have conducted [*legal research or investigation*] to determine whether or not we felt you had a claim that could be asserted against [*insert appropriate name(s)*].

The result of our [*research/investigation*] indicates that there is not an enforceable legal basis for maintaining an action against [*insert appropriate name(s)*].

(optional paragraph)

Our opinion is based upon our preliminary research; however, we have found [*insert number*] cases that support our conclusion.

We urge you to consult another lawyer if you wish to obtain a second opinion. Time limitations may affect your rights to pursue a claim; therefore, you should act promptly in consulting another lawyer or otherwise pursuing your claim.

At this time, however, we are unable to proceed on your behalf. We are returning your original documents to you.

Thank you for your interest in our firm.

Very truly yours,

[*signature*]

Enclosures

Reference: LOMAS, The Florida Bar, *Administrative Forms Handbook*.
Reprinted with permission.

EXAMPLE 4-7: DISENGAGEMENT LETTER—UNPAID FEES

DATE

NAME
ADDRESS
CITY, STATE & ZIP

Dear:

During the past [*time*], it has been our pleasure to serve you as counsel in [*subject matter title*]. In the course of that representation, you have paid us [*dollar amount already paid*] in legal fees and expenses. Unfortunately, contrary to our Engagement Agreement, you have not paid our statements in a timely manner for the past few months.

At this time, the outstanding and overdue fees and expenses total approximately [*dollar amount currently owing*]. Our firm desires to continue our relationship, but does not have the ability to finance your case. Moreover, you expressly agreed that the hourly fees and expenses in this matter would be kept current.

We have continued to represent you for the past [*time*], even though each month the outstanding fees and expenses increased. We did so because we value our relationship with you and would like to continue representing you.

At this point, in our opinion, the trial court will permit us to withdraw. There is still sufficient time for you to retain other counsel without jeopardizing your case or adversely affecting the court's calendar. However, if we wait several more months, it is possible that one of these conditions for withdrawal may not exist.

Your new counsel may wish to discuss this case with us. That would be to your advantage both substantively and economically. We are willing to do so as long as satisfactory arrangements are made to compensate us for the additional time and expense which will be incurred. In addition, it will be necessary to agree on a plan to gradually reduce the outstanding fees and expenses. We also have certain work product which has been generated during the past [*time*]. We are willing to share it with your new counsel to the extent our legal obligations require us to do so in the absence of full payment of our fees and expenses.

I enclose a petition for withdrawal which will be filed with the court ten days from your receipt of this letter. In the meantime, if you wish us to continue representing you, we would be pleased to do so if satisfactory arrangements are made to take care of the outstanding and overdue fees and expenses, as well as to take care of the future fees and expenses. I look forward to hearing from you, and remain hopeful the representation can continue.

Very truly yours,

[*signature*]

Reference: LOMAS, The Florida Bar, *Administrative Forms Handbook.* Reprinted with permission.

EXAMPLE 4-8:
INITIAL CLIENT CONSULTATION INTERVIEW FORM

The purpose of an initial consultation is for the attorney to advise you, the *prospective* client, what, if anything, may be done for you, and what the minimum fee therefore will be. *The purpose is not to render a definitive legal opinion,* as it may be impossible to fully assess a matter within the time frame allotted for a consultation or with the (information or documents) that you may be able to provide at the initial consultation.

One of three outcomes is possible following your consultation.

A. **You and the Attorney mutually agree to the terms of representation, or** (After a separate document called an Agreement for Representation is signed, a copy will be provided to you.)
B. **The Attorney declines representation, or**
C. **You decide not to use the services of the Attorney.**

Note: The following questions will help us to understand the reason for your visit today. Your responses are protected by attorney/client privilege and will be held in strict confidence.

Name_____
       Last   First   Middle or Maiden

Address_____
       Number   Street   City   State   Zip

Home Phone (___)_____   Cell Phone (___)_____

E-Mail Address_____

Briefly explain what you need advice about or assistance with today:

_____

_____

_____

Are there other parties involved? (Examples: a friend, an employer, a neighbor, signor of a contract, etc. This should include people or parties on either side of your issue.)

Party_____ Relationship_____

Party_____ Relationship_____

Party_____ Relationship_____

On the lines below, list the documents (papers) that you think may help us to understand the issues.

(1)_____

(2)_____

(3)_____
(NOTE: *Any documents you supply that are important to your matter will be photocopied or scanned, with your permission, and your originals returned to you at the conclusion of the initial interview.*)

Ideally, if things turn out precisely the way you want, what would the outcome be?

_____

_____

Knowing that there are no guarantees, what can you accept?

_____

_____

Please classify your urgency in concluding this matter. (Check One)
[ ]   Critical—Personal safety or continuation of business depends on it.
[ ]   Very important—Severe hardship, personal or financial inconvenience if matter is not resolved quickly.
[ ]   Important—Matter interferes with business or personal financial stability.
[ ]   Needs to be done, but no immediate hardship in the interim.
[ ]   Just thought I'd see if it was worth pursuing, but I'm not counting on anything.
[ ]   Just wanted to know what my rights are. I'll then let you know after I think about it.

If the matter involves payment to you of money you feel you are owed, how long can you wait before not getting paid?

_____
(Days, Weeks, Months, Years)

Are we the first attorneys you have consulted regarding this matter?
[ ] Yes   [ ] No

If No—Why didn't you hire their services? _____

_____

Have you ever been represented by an attorney before? [ ] Yes [ ] No

If Yes—Please state the circumstances _____

_____

How will you pay for your attorney's fees in this matter?

[ ] Check today [ ] Cash today [ ] Contingency Fee [ ] On Account

[ ] Credit Card _____ _____

                               Credit Card No.   Expr. Date

Marital Status: [ ] Married [ ] Single [ ] Divorced [ ] Widowed [ ] Separated

Driver's License # _____

Social Security # _____ _____ _____

Are you known by any other names? [ ] Yes [ ] No

If yes what name(s)_____
(A fictitious name, a nickname, a former name, your maiden name, etc.)

Where are you employed? _____

May we contact you there? [ ] Yes [ ] No

Phone # (_____)_____

If your mail is returned as undeliverable or your telephone service terminated, please provide the name of someone (friend or relative) you believe will always know how to contact you.

Name_____

Relationship _____

Address_____
          Number   Street   City   State   Zip

Phone #s (_____)_____

How did you learn of our office? [ ] A friend [ ] Our Web Page/Internet Search [ ] Bar Referral [ ] Former or current client [ ] Other

PLEASE READ CAREFULLY & Sign Below

Following your initial interview, if you agree to hire the Attorney, and the Attorney agrees to represent you, you will both sign an Agreement for Representation. The Agreement for Representation will set forth the terms and conditions of representation.

If the Attorney is willing to represent you and you decide not to sign an Agreement of Representation today, you are strongly urged to schedule a second appointment with the Attorney at the earliest possible time or to immediately consult with other legal counsel to protect your rights.

NOTICE: This office does not represent you with regard to the matters set forth by you herein in this information sheet or discussed during your consultation, <u>unless and until</u> both you and the Attorney execute a written Agreement for Representation.

If the Attorney does not agree to represent you, this includes not representing you with regard to the matter set forth by you on this information sheet, or any other matters you may discuss with the Attorney during your consultation. If your legal problem(s) involve a potential lawsuit, it is important that you realize a lawsuit must be filed within a certain period of time called a Statute of Limitations. Therefore, the Attorney strongly urges you to *immediately* consult with another attorney to protect your rights. The Attorney's decision not to represent you should not be taken by you as an expression regarding the merits of your case.

Your signature acknowledges <u>only that you received a copy</u> of this completed information sheet and does not mean you have hired the Attorney.

SIGNATURE _____ Date ___/___/___

****

This portion to be completed by the Attorney

[ ]   Will represent (See New Case Memo and Agreement for Representation attached).
[ ]   Will investigate and report (Schedule a follow-up conference for ____days).
[ ]   Representation declined - Letter of declination will be sent.
[ ]   Party will "think about it" and get back with us - No action to be taken and party was so informed.
[ ]   Client declined Representation at this time.

Interviewed by _____ this ___ day of _____, _____

Notes:_____
_____
_____
_____
_____
_____
_____
_____

The Quality of Your Practice Is Equal to the Quality of Your Clients

As you can see, the quality of your practice is determined largely by the quality of your clients. Imagine how different your practice would be if you worked with nothing but A- and B-level clients. You might actually look forward to going into the office in the morning! They pay their bills, appreciate the value of the work you do for them, cooperate with you, show up on time, and send quality referrals. These are clients you can actually enjoy. They are not completely crisis-driven, and they trust your opinion. These are the clients who can get lost in the shuffle when you must scramble to handle the constant demands of your C and D clients. Every negative characteristic you can attach to clients means more time you will have to spend persuading them to trust you, calming them down, or trying to get paid.

Carefully selecting the clients you work with not only helps protect you against malpractice accusations, it also has the added benefit of saving you precious time, improving office morale, minimizing collection problems, and restoring peace in an otherwise crisis-driven practice. To better manage yourself, your time, and your practice, develop your client selection skills. The impact will be significant.

APPENDIX #2

Proactive Strategy Seven: Manage Interruptions

You'll never be able to successfully implement the time template we've just described unless you develop a proactive approach to managing interruptions. In this chapter, we present preemptive strikes for avoiding interruptions altogether, give you some tips for handling them, and help you identify the sources of the interruptions in your office.

Industrial engineers have determined that the average length of an interruption is seven minutes, and it takes about three minutes to get back into what you were doing when you were interrupted. This adds up to 10 minutes per interruption. Six interruptions occur and you have lost an hour; 12 interruptions and you've lost two hours. Many attorneys experience 20 or more interruptions on an easy day.

Many attorneys don't start serious production until after five in the afternoon, when the office quiets down and they can concentrate. They work from five o'clock until eight, nine or later, all the while feeling bad about not spending time with the family or pursuing life outside their practice. It is not uncommon for us to hear attorneys say they view Saturdays and even Sundays as a real haven—not for rest and relaxation, but to concentrate and get work done. When they analyze this statement, they realize it is primarily because there are no interruptions to deal with. However, what they have gained in time spent on production is a huge loss in the personal column of life, interacting with family as well as taking care of themselves. Attorneys who operate this way must then squeeze their so-called personal life into the few hours that remain of the weekend—that is, if they have the energy. Is it any wonder that the failure rate of attorney marriages is so high?

Create Critical Interruption Criteria

Maybe 20% of the interruptions you experience are valid, time-sensitive, and truly important enough to displace whatever you are working on. The remaining 80% of the interruptions can and should be handled at other times and in structured ways. Two proactive methods to help you get a handle on the interruptions in your office are as follows:

- Create standards for what *truly* constitutes a valid interruption during your production time.
- Create a list of allowable interruptions.

"The average American worker has 50 interruptions a day, of which 70% have nothing to do with work."
—W. Edward Deming

Start by creating, with your staff, a list of typical client crises or emergency scenarios that get your attention when and if they occur. This is a very useful list to help staff distinguish the real emergencies from the false ones. Staff members who are new and not seasoned may believe that every client problem must be immediately elevated to the attorney instead of tactfully handing the client over to the designated hitter, who may be able to help. This is especially true of a new staff person who has never worked in a law practice before and doesn't realize the emotional instability of some clients who often want extra attention or just someone to talk to. A discussion of real emergencies you have dealt with in the past can be very valuable. We are not trying to downplay the validity of the problems the client may be having; sometimes the client can be satisfied only by talking to you. Sometimes you must immediately respond to something that the opposing counsel, a judge, or a partner has done. There are plenty of legitimate emergencies among those masquerading as such. It is important for you and your staff to clarify the difference. The interruptions at issue are those that can be diverted so that you have protected time for production during the day and not after hours.

Set Criteria for What Constitutes an Emergency

Another way to establish guidelines regarding emergencies and interruptions is to make a list of "allowable interrupters." Your spouse and some family members are usually on the list of people who may interrupt your production time if they have something urgent to discuss. If you have school-age children, the schools should be able to interrupt with urgent messages. You can institute a standing list for your staff and include your spouse, your children's schools, a couple of trusted friends, and even some A+ clients. Some offices make a changing list on a daily basis, which they e-mail or instant message to the call screener. For example, the call screener knows that your spouse and certain other individuals can always get through; otherwise, today's list of allowable calls is limited to those whose files you are currently addressing in your production time. So if you are going to be working on the Smith file and the Jones file today, Mrs. Smith and Mr. Jones are allowed to interrupt. Other than that, you may have a small list of important clients or influencers who get your attention whenever they call. This list should be small and select.

Case Study
Time Management Issue: Handling Emergency Interruptions

Attorney: Divorce Attorney
State: New York

This matrimonial attorney provides us with a great example of the challenge of handling certain interruptions. One morning, she was in court on a case that went on longer than she'd anticipated. It finally concluded at noon. She had planned to drive to Amherst, Massachusetts that afternoon to attend an important event with her family. Scheduled to leave her office for the trip at 1:00, she planned on going home, packing, and then getting on the road by 2:00. Before her departure, however, a long-standing client came in with an emergency that involved the welfare of a child. Immediately, she put her plans on hold, sat down with the client, calmed her, and discussed the appropriate legal action to take. Weighing her options, she decided to complete as much work as she could before she got on the road, and promised the client she'd continue working on the case during the day via cell phone.

By this point, her schedule was thrown totally off and continued to get worse. She was stuck in heavy traffic and arrived just as the event was ending, much to the disappointment of her family. Instead of the relaxing family gathering she'd planned, her day was filled with stress, frustration and disappointment.

Atticus Tip:
There is no way to schedule every moment and avoid being faced with authentic emergency interruptions at times. She had done everything right. She had scheduled time to spend with her family, allowed time for the court appearance in case it ran late, and given herself some margin back at the office before she set out on her drive. She never planned, however, to deal with such a time-consuming interruption. On this day, she had to make

difficult choices and pushed her own interests aside in favor of the client's. At times, this is the appropriate choice. The important thing is this: Make this type of scenario a memorable event that you can learn from, and not a typical routine in your office. If you find yourself routinely making choices that further your client's interests and fail to take care of your own, you will begin to resent your clients and despise the practice of law. Try to preempt client crises as much as possible, and begin to overestimate the time needed to accomplish your daily goals so you can absorb the unexpected.

To begin to get a handle on managing interruptions, let's break them down into categories:

- Family and friends who drop by or call
- Office socializing
- Staff, partner and client interruptions
- The "self-interrupting" work style

Handling Interruptions from Family and Friends

Interruptions that may come from your personal life—kids, family or friends— can be managed. The solution lies in redirection.

- Let personal callers know not to call during your production time.
- Direct (or have your call screener direct) personal callers to call during your lunch hour if you plan to eat at your desk.
- Direct your call screener to ask callers if you can call them back after your production time.

Just as you can retrain your staff and co-workers to support your efforts in managing your time, you can let important people in your personal life know that you are trying to be more efficient during the day so that you have more time to be with them in the evenings and on the weekends.

Handling Socializing and Work Interruptions

Let's begin by giving you some quick tips for preempting or shortening socializing and work interruptions. It may be as simple as adopting a new set of nonverbal clues, shifting your body language, or simply making a change in the physical setup of your office. Notice that these tips for "taming" interruptions apply to both work and social situations, as the circumstances causing an interruption inevitably overlap.

- **Use a Visual Cue**

  One attorney we know keeps a photo of his family on his desk. This attorney, because of his warm nature, has been plagued with co-workers who take up a lot of his time discussing their personal problems. Since becoming aware that he is spending a lot of time in unproductive conversation, he has established a quick trigger to remind himself of his goals. He looks at the co-worker, looks at the picture of his kids, and asks himself, "Would I rather spend time talking to this person and end up working late, or see my kids before they go to bed tonight?" Without fail, he chooses the kids. This has been a great source of motivation for him.

- **Let's Do Lunch**

  Corral co-workers to join you for lunch. You are preempting social interruptions by catching up on each other's news and adding a bit of fun and relaxation as well.

- **Tell Them You Prefer E-mail**

  E-mail offers a great alternative to face-to-face and phone conversations because you can answer at an appropriately scheduled time. Internal e-mail is also a great way for staff to batch questions, which you can answer at an appropriate time.

- **Get Creative with Your Communication Methods**

  Conference calls are great for group communication. One hour spent communicating with a group of three beats three hours communicating one message to three people. Most telephone companies have extended conference-calling services available. One such service, called a bridge line, allows you to put up to 150 people on the same call at the same time. The approach can be useful for much smaller groups as well, especially for meetings that may not warrant travel but involve critical participants from different locations.

  Communicating by e-mail is a timesaving device. It allows you to put all of your thoughts down in a coherent fashion, which can then be sent to as many people as necessary. This leverages your time by allowing you to communicate to many people simultaneously.

- **Let Your Body Do the Talking**

  When you see someone entering your office with whom you do not want to get into a long conversation, stand up. This cues them in a nonverbal fashion that you are in a hurry or on your way out. If that doesn't slow them down, actually walk toward the door and leave (even if you just walk to the restroom). In addition, when you want to end a conversation, break off eye contact with the other person. They will feel that it is time to leave without your having to say a word.

- **Play Musical Chairs**
  Move the visitors' chairs in your office away from your desk when you are not seeing clients. Make your office a little less comfortable for chatting. When the chairs are not conveniently placed at your desk, people are more likely to stand, and consequently their time with you becomes shorter.

- **Don't Catch Their Eye**
  Move your desk so that you are not in view of the passing traffic in the office. If people can easily see you and catch your eye, they are more likely to come in and socialize.

- **Close Your Door and Mean It**
  Enroll your staff in the idea that when you shut your door, you are not to be disturbed by anyone (except for those on the list). This is critical to your production time. If the rest of the office does not respect your closed door, send out an e-mail saying that you are committed to managing interruptions so you can be more productive. Mention that your secretary can help anyone in the office who needs to speak to you (unless it is a *true* emergency). As you begin to take your time seriously, so do others. Example 7-1 is a sample of a closed-door policy you could issue in the form of an e-mail.

EXAMPLE 7-1: E-MAIL ON CLOSED-DOOR POLICY

In an attempt to manage my time better and concentrate on high-priority projects, I'll be closing my door every day between the hours of 9:00 and 11:00 a.m., starting immediately. During this time, I won't be seeing anyone or taking any incoming phone calls; all incoming calls will be returned between the hours of 11:00 and 12:00 so that clients are taken care of quickly. *(If you have an assistant or designated hitter in place, you can mention that they will be handling the calls at this time.)*

This new schedule will help me eliminate the late nights and weekends I have spent trying to get caught up. If you have questions for me, we can meet before or after my production time or you may e-mail them to me at any time.

Thanks for your cooperation.

- **Tame the Telephone**
  The telephone can be a major source of interruptions. Practice good time management on the telephone by using the following tips:

  - When initiating a call that you want to keep short, set up the expectation that the conversation will be a quick one right from the start:
    > "Hi, Dan, I only have a moment, but I wanted to give you a quick call about . . ."
    >
    > "Hi, Karen, I know you're busy, but I just wanted to give you a quick call to let you know that . . ."
  - When receiving a call that you want to keep short, you can also set up the expectation at the beginning that it will be brief:
    > "Hi, Joe, I was just on my way out . . ."
    >
    > "Hello, Jane. Unfortunately, I've only got a minute to talk. What can I help you with?"

Statistics show that socializing accounts for 80% of unnecessary interruptions. If you view this in terms of loss of production and loss of personal time, you begin to view the problem as one that needs to be dealt with, not just regarded as annoying. Human beings are social animals, and socializing is important on many levels. It is unrealistic and unhealthy to eliminate socializing altogether. The strong internal rapport and sense of teamwork that a well-run office possesses is built and maintained this way. By adopting the quick tips listed herein, you are becoming proactive in a way that results in a work environment in which office socializing is valued but is not intrusive or a constant distraction.

Handling Staff, Partners, and Client Interruptions

Work-related interruptions can come from many sources. We focus on the three sources that are the most problematic: your staff, your clients, and (if you have them), your partners.

Staff-Related Interruptions

Lurk and blurt: One of the major causes of work-related interruptions is staff members who do not feel they have enough time with you to get their questions answered. We touched on this in Chapter 6, where we emphasized how important it is to schedule a regular time for your staff to meet with you. In lieu of a regularly scheduled meeting time, your staff will interrupt you because they perceive that you are too busy or distracted to meet with them.

They've stooped to the "lurking and blurting" technique to be able to get the information they need so that they can move on with their task. This means they lurk outside your office door and rush in saying, "I just have to ask you one quick question," or "I just need five minutes of your time." These interruptions are never as quick and easy as you or they like to believe, and they can derail you dramatically. It is not fair to either you or your staff to work like this. Nevertheless, most offices run on the lurking and blurting concept. We encourage you to eliminate that behavior if it exists in your office, because it disrespects your time—the most expensive time in the office—and weakens the time template system.

> **"Remember the plate-spinner on the old Ed Sullivan Show? I'm him. That's how I feel with all the cases I am juggling, constantly running back and forth just trying to give everything enough of a spin to keep it from crashing to the floor."**
> **—*Atticus client***

Solution: You can solve this problem by giving staff a reliable meeting time, institutionalized on your time template and theirs, and sticking to it faithfully. If you follow the three-part formula for your production time block, you always meet with staff right before or right after your session behind closed doors. Reinforce the idea of batching, explaining that a batched group of 10 questions presented in one sitting may eliminate 10 interruptions during the course of the day. Also, stick to your commitment to batch your questions for them for the same reasons.

I can't do this without you: The second reason your staff may be a source of constant interruptions is that they are untrained and truly don't know how to do anything in the office without your constant supervision.

Solution: You can solve this problem by providing more training for your staff. If you don't have the time to train them yourself, assign someone else to do it. If you don't have anyone else who can train them, send them to seminars for paralegals and legal assistants. Give them materials. Even if some of the materials are meant for attorneys, your staff may be able to glean some helpful information from them.

You may run into a situation in which a staff person cannot be trained despite your most valiant efforts. We suggest you replace this individual with an experienced person. One of the worst things that a very busy attorney can do is to hire a staff person who knows absolutely nothing of the attorney's practice area just because he or she is inexpensive. These individuals require a significant investment of time and training early on to see if they are even going to be an asset to the firm. When you are extremely busy or know that you can't take the time to train a new hire, do yourself a favor and hire staff with at least a medium level of experience so you don't have to watch every move they make. You save yourself in time what it would have cost you to get an inexperienced hire up to speed.

Client-Related Interruptions

Your clients are another common source of interruptions, but they don't have to be. Look at the following list of challenges attorneys typically encounter and examine the solutions that reduce these interruptions:

Just a quick question: Your clients call you constantly with "quick" questions or because they need "handholding." Every day, you spend hours on the phone reassuring clients and not necessarily discussing substantive matters.

Solution: Use your first client meeting to clarify information about your schedule and office protocol for the best way to contact you, including:

- The time of day you are most likely to be reached
- When you are usually in court (if applicable)
- The name and contact information of your "designated hitter"

A word of caution: It is best to avoid giving clients too much access to you by giving out your home phone or cell phone number. It is acceptable and understandable at times to give these numbers out when you have a true emergency situation, but if you give them out on a regular basis, people subvert your production time by calling/texting you on your cell phone. They track you down after hours with questions that could easily wait until business hours. Try not to contaminate your personal time with unfettered access. You'll eventually resent your clients for invading your privacy and feel even more enslaved by your practice.

Of all of these preemptive strikes against interruptions, using a designated hitter is the most advantageous way of eliminating many interruptions. We talked about the designated hitter's importance in determining the success of the time template in Chapter 6. Here, we continue to emphasize the role of the designated hitter when you are trying to conquer the problem of interruptions.

If you can get the designated hitter to bond with the client, most of the questions will go to the designated hitter, not to you. Anything that the designated hitter does not know the answer to, or cannot legally answer, can be brought to your attention, and you can get back to the client or, better yet, the designated hitter can relay your response to the client. In this way, you have included another friendly face in the access chain, and it frees you up from a considerable number of phone calls, e-mails and face-to-face meetings.

Stop! I'm in crisis!: These folks are probably the ones who showed up at your office, already in crisis, wanting you to drop everything and take care of them immediately. These are the individuals who have probably used two or three attorneys before you. Once you have taken on these clients, you find that your practice is drawn into constant crisis mode along with them.

Solution: Take a proactive stance and be very selective about the clients you take on, as we discussed in Chapter 5. You may need to review the key points concerning client selection and view it through the perspective of its usefulness in limiting or eliminating interruptions. Don't revert to being reactive and work with any client who shows up on your doorstep. When a new client is sitting before you, really evaluate whether he or she is likely to cause constant crises. You can preempt a lot of interruptions, potential chaos, and emotional upheaval in your office by not taking these people on. If you are ever in doubt about whether a potential client is a C- or D-level client, consult with your staff. They can spot bad clients from miles away.

Partners who "lurk and blurt" can be tamed: You may also have interruptions in the form of a partner, or partners, who barge into your office at all times with questions or comments, oblivious to the fact that you are trying to concentrate. They may be trying to discuss important staffing issues, address administrative problems, or simply want to use you as a sounding board for an idea. These partners are showing symptoms of a shortage of reliable meeting time with you to get their questions answered and to discuss important issues. They may have stooped to the "lurking and blurting" technique just to get time with you. In our experience, many firms are managed in a completely ad hoc fashion by two or more partners who have no structured partner's meeting.

Solution: Give your partners a reliable meeting time. Create a once-a-week or twice-a-month partner's meeting. Make attendance mandatory. Institutionalize it in your time template and in theirs, and stick to it faithfully. Teach them to batch their questions and organize a standing agenda that devotes time to the following areas:

- Finance/bookkeeping issues
- Staffing issues, firing and hiring

- Administrative/technology issues
- Marketing plans

Look at Example 7-2, which shows a meeting agenda containing these areas that can assist you and your partners in making meeting time productive. Complete and distribute this form at least 24 hours prior to the meeting to allow partners sufficient time to prepare. Many firms that we work with have a partner's lunch on Monday after a morning meeting with the bookkeeper.

EXAMPLE 7-2: PARTNER'S MEETING AGENDA

Agenda Items   Notes

1. **Finance** (include bookkeeper when appropriate)
   - ❑ 📁 Review Dashboard and/or A/R, A/P, P&L reports
   - ❑ 📄 Discuss collection issues
   - ❑ 📄 Discuss cashflow projections for upcoming month, quarter
   - ❑ 📄 Discuss productivity, timekeeping, bookkeeping, billing issues
   - ❑ 📄 Approve large purchases, monitor budget variances
   - ❑ ⌛ Other:_____
   - ❑ 📧 Action items:_____
     - Who:_____By when:_____
   - ❑ 📧 Action items:_____
     - Who:_____By when:_____
   - ❑ 📧 Action items:_____
     - Who:_____By when:_____

2. **Staffing**   Notes
   - ❑ 📁 Discuss personnel problems, upcoming reviews
   - ❑ 📄 Discuss plans to fill open positions, vacation coverage
   - ❑ 📄 Discuss training to be conducted
   - ❑ 📄 Discuss employee benefits
   - ❑ ⌛ Other:_____
   - ❑ 📁📁 Action items:_____
     - Who:_____By when:_____
   - ❑ 📁📁 Action items:_____
     - Who:_____By when:_____
   - ❑ 📁📄 Action items:_____
     - Who:_____By when:_____

3. **Client Development**   Notes

    ❑ 📁 Set monthly marketing goals (include charitable and
    community sponsorships)

    ❑ 📄 Discuss media, advertising or PR opportunities

    ❑ 📄 Discuss client service goals, client retention issues

    ❑ 📰 Review number of referrals, compare to goal, discuss
    follow-up actions

    ❑ ⏳ Other:_____

    ❑ 📠 Action items:_____
       Who:_____By when:_____

    ❑ 📠 Action items:_____
       Who:_____By when:_____

    ❑ 📠 Action items:_____
       Who:_____By when:_____

    ❑ 📁 Action items:_____
       Who:_____By when:_____

4. **Technology**   Notes

    ❑ 📁 Discuss hardware, software, phone system, website
    needs or issues

    ❑ 📄 Discuss possible upgrades to hardware or software

    ❑ 📄 Review and/or plan technology training needs for staff
    and attorneys

    ❑ ⏳ Other:_____

    ❑ 📠 Action items:_____
       Who:_____By when:_____

    ❑ 📠 Action items:_____
       Who:_____By when:_____

    ❑ 📠 Action items:_____
       Who:_____By when:_____

5. **Administrative/Operations Projects**   Notes

    ❑ 📁 Review facilities, space-planning issues and concerns

    ❑ 📄 Discuss office equipment needs, issues

    ❑ 📄 Discuss research on large expenditures, discuss supply
    problems

    ❑ 📄 Discuss policies and procedures issues

    ❑ ⏳ Other:_____

    ❑ 📠 Action items:_____
       Who:_____By when:_____

    ❑ 📠 Action items:_____
       Who:_____By when:_____

    ❑ 📠 Action items:_____
       Who:_____By when:_____

Are You a Self-Interrupting Attorney?

We have talked about the annoying and costly interruptions of others, but, like many attorneys, you may be the source of many of your own interruptions. You are most likely to be a self-interrupter if you exhibit some of the characteristics we have attributed to the reactive style of management:

- Driven by adrenaline
- Have a short attention span
- Driven by deadlines (won't act until up against a deadline)
- Easily bored
- Pride yourself on your ability to multi-task

If you fall into one or more of the reactive-style management categories just listed, you may also find that you can relate to these behaviors as well:

- Not only do you interrupt yourself, but you tend to interrupt others.
- You've gotten out of the habit of focusing your attention for longer than 10 or 20 minutes.
- When you close your door to go into your production time, you feel cut off and isolated from the office.
- You want to do anything but work on the files or documents that you have planned to work on. Instead, you feel a tremendous urge to do something else:
  - Pick up the telephone
  - Look at e-mail
  - Write an e-mail
  - Work on a different file
  - Search the Internet
  - Stare out the window
  - Rearrange your desk
  - Catch up on your reading
  - Consult with your partners
  - Read the newspaper
  - Give more instructions to your staff
  - Get a cup of coffee
  - Get a glass of water
  - Engage in texting

- Take a restroom break
- Get a snack

The seemingly innocent urges in this last list are what resistance looks like. These urges are your habitual ways of operating conspiring against you. Trying to set up new habits of focusing your attention during your production time is challenging. When you close your door, you may feel lonely and cut off from the rest of the office, and crave some outside form of stimulation. You won't be very focused initially, and you'll want to do anything but the files or projects that you have assigned yourself to work on. These feelings are all normal, so don't give in. It is up to you to prevail over the hold your old habits have over you.

Solutions for Self-Interrupters

Keep a legal pad handy. One solution is to keep a legal pad handy when you go into production time. The idea is to have a place to capture all of those thoughts that arise to pull you off track during your power-hour time. As all of these urgent, self-interrupting thoughts pop into your mind, simply write them down. If any of the urges are tasks that you really must do, you have captured them on your legal pad and they are then easily transferred to your to-do list after your production time is over.

Time yourself and take a break. If you notice that you cannot concentrate for longer than 20 minutes, set yourself up to work on a project for 20 minutes, and then take a five-minute break, but stay in your office. Give yourself something to do—a quick phone call, for example. Do not leave your office unless you absolutely have to, because you will get pulled farther off track. After your break, either pick up something else to work on or return to the first task and work for another 20 minutes. During the beginning weeks of committing to your production time, knowing you have a break every 20 minutes will help you. The following week, try to concentrate for 25 or 30 minutes at a stretch. In this way you can train yourself to concentrate for longer and longer periods as you raise the bar each week.

Get creative with ways to focus. Experiment to figure out how you can leverage yourself into action. For example, some of our attorney clients know that they are the bottlenecks for paperwork in the office. They use this knowledge to leverage themselves into focusing. Work that they must review comes into their in-box and stays there for weeks at a time. The staff are frustrated, waiting for them to review the work before they can proceed to completion. To resolve this situation, these attorneys use the first hour of their production time to review work. This structured approach gives them confidence that they can keep the staff moving on their assigned tasks. Once the review is done, the attorneys concentrate on their own highest-priority production.

One attorney had difficulty making herself go through her case files to get the work moving. We asked her to bring in her assistant for 45 minutes with the stated goal of sorting through all the files together and identifying the work that could be delegated. She was pleasantly surprised to find that teaming up with another person and discussing each file was a creative and effective way to deal with her resistance to this chore.

Some attorneys prefer to review work in the afternoons between client appointments. The key is to learn creative ways that keep you on task and focused. Look at the backlogged work in your office. Decide whether you need to focus on it more formally, and include it in your production time or some other slot on your time template.

Celebrate your small victories. We've worked with many attorneys with short attention spans who initially resisted the power-hour idea. After improving their ability to concentrate, they cling to their closed-door production time as the most important time of their day. They've learned to honor their commitments to themselves. Commit to yourself that you will develop the ability to focus for longer and longer periods. Reward yourself for keeping your commitments.

Managing the Biggest Interruption of All: The Trial

If you are a trial attorney (skip this section if you do not have a trial practice) and have committed to moving toward a proactive approach to time management, the period of time surrounding a trial will be a true test of your ability to stick to that commitment. In many practices, we have witnessed the trial preparation period and the trial period turn into *one big interruption*. The temptation is strong for adrenaline-driven lawyers and irresistible to those with reactive tendencies. The solution is to stick to a reduced time template. This reduced template includes trial-related tasks put into blocks. Consequently, your office is not turned upside down and you remain focused on the trial as well as steady at the helm of your practice responsibilities. Examples 7-3 and 7-4 set forth trial time templates, Option A and B, to give you some guidance on creating one in your practice.

EXAMPLE 7-3: SAMPLE TRIAL TIME TEMPLATE—OPTION A

This modified time template is to help you organize your time in trial, while still tending to the important issues pending with other clients. It allows for an early-morning meeting with your staff to handle trial delegation and non-trial-related client updates. After your day in court there is time for returning phone calls, e-mails and texts to the most important non-trial-related clients. The day after trial (we have four days pictured; your actual trial may be longer or shorter) is scheduled as a "Phantom Day." This day allows for some recovery time. No client appointments or outside phone calls are scheduled on this day. The attorney is in the office only to catch up on work that has accumulated while in trial.

	MONDAY	TUESDAY	WEDNESDAY	THURSDAY	FRIDAY
9:00 a.m.	STAFF MEETING	MORNING STAFF MEETING PRIOR TO COURT			
10:00 a.m.		APPROXIMATE TIME IN COURTHOUSE (THIS TIME WILL BE SHORTER OR LONGER DEPENDING ON THE ACTUAL DURATION OF THE TRIAL)			PHANTOM DAY
11:00 a.m.					
12:00 p.m.					
1:00 p.m.					
2:00 p.m.					
3:00 p.m.					
4:00 p.m.					
5:00 p.m.					
6:00 p.m.	LATE AFTERNOON MEETINGS/RETURN NON-TRIAL-RELATED PHONE CALLS, E-MAILS, TEXTS				

EXAMPLE 7-4: SAMPLE TRIAL TIME TEMPLATE—OPTION B

As this trial begins on Tuesday, it allows for a weekly planning session on Monday and a staff meeting prior to a full day of preparation. While in trial, an early-morning meeting with your staff to handle trial delegation and non-trial-related client updates is scheduled. After your day in court, there is time for returning phone calls, e-mails and texts to the most important non-trial-related clients. The day after trial (we have three days pictured; your actual trial may be longer or shorter) is scheduled as a "Phantom Day" to allow for some recovery time. No client appointments or outside phone calls are scheduled on this day. The attorney is in the office only to catch up on work that has accumulated while in trial.

	MONDAY	TUESDAY	WEDNESDAY	THURSDAY	FRIDAY
9:00 a.m.	STAFF MEETING	MORNING STAFF MEETING PRIOR TO COURT			
10:00 a.m.	TRIAL PREP	APPROXIMATE TIME IN COURTHOUSE (THIS TIME WILL BE SHORTER OR LONGER DEPENDING ON THE ACTUAL DURATION OF THE TRIAL)			PHANTOM DAY
11:00 a.m.					
12:00 p.m.					
1:00 p.m.					
2:00 p.m.					
3:00 p.m.					
4:00 p.m.					
5:00 p.m.					
6:00 p.m.	RETURN PHONE CALLS	LATE AFTERNOON MEETINGS/RETURN NON-TRIAL-RELATED PHONE CALLS, E-MAILS AND TEXTS			

Resist the Reactive Approach When Preparing for Trial

The reactive approach is not an uncommon approach among attorneys who have something of an adrenaline addiction. It is caused by knowing that if you wait long enough, you can rely on the adrenaline boost to carry you through those final days and nights of intense preparation. That's when you lock yourself away—eating, sleeping, and thinking of nothing other than the case. You eventually emerge, bleary-eyed, to go forth and try the case. If you win, this whirlwind preparation style is dramatically reinforced. If you lose, you vow to never do it again, but then quite often do. The cycle continues even though you end up hating yourself for this reactive and repetitive behavior.

> **"Time flies. It's up to you to be the navigator."**
> **—Robert Orben**

Proactively Plan and Schedule

Some of your trial preparation has to wait until the last minute, when you are certain the trial really will happen. However, it is possible to jump-start the process. Take those items that can be worked on early and either schedule yourself or someone else to begin working on them. Your proactive approach includes two main goals:

- Anticipate what you need well in advance, and
- Block time early to prepare for it.

Create a Trial Notebook

Three weeks before a trial is not too soon to begin anticipating what you need. One of the critical elements of this preparation is the **trial notebook**. Ideally, you already have a systemized approach to putting a trial notebook together. If not, you can use the notebook for your current trial as the model for notebooks in the future, or you can use your word-processing software to file your table of contents checklist on your computer for future use.

A systemized trial notebook includes a checklist, a diagram of a notebook, or an actual model notebook to use as reference. You or your staff member can create a detailed table of contents listing every form and document that is typically used. All of your tabs are standardized based on your table of contents and can be made up ahead of time. This detailed table of contents can serve double-duty as the notebook assembly checklist. You can have a staff member begin assembling the notebook so that you can begin filling it up early in the process. Get as much help as you can to start putting the trial notebook together early so that all the work doesn't have to happen the week before trial.

Block the Time for Trial-Related Events

Once your trial notebook has been set in motion, focus on blocking time for all things related to the trial. If you do not block time for it on your time template and your calendar, you will be tempted to bump other work for trial-related activities. Because a fair amount of preparation must occur the week before or several days before the trial, you should try to dedicate all of your production time on those days to trial preparation. Below is a chronological list of activities that should occur as soon as the trial date is set:

1. Block out the trial and several days prior on your calendar.
2. Work backwards and start blocking additional preparation time.
3. Block the day after the trial as a "Phantom Day for recovery."

Staff should automatically block out the days prior to the trial on the calendar to ensure your ability to focus. Have them schedule time by working backwards and blocking additional preparation time up to three weeks before the trial. When lawyers prepare for trial, they go into "hyper-focus" mode. They go behind closed doors, don't allow any interruptions, and really concentrate. We encourage the intensity of this mode, but not the drama and irritability that surround it when it is crammed into the week before trial. Negative feelings result when you become cranky and irritable with staff members, partners, and clients. The solution is to get into hyper-focus mode prior to the week before trial by scheduling an hour or two each day in the three weeks leading up to the trial.

In the week before the trial, continue to conduct your weekly planning session at the beginning of the week. Continue your daily staff meetings so that you can monitor what is happening in the rest of your practice. Take at least an hour to review work that your staff completes in order to keep the work flowing. During your trial, try to maintain a skeletal version of your time template that includes a quick meeting with staff, either on the phone or in person, on a daily basis. Refer to Examples 7-3 and 7-4 to see how this works.

The day after the trial should be blocked as a "Phantom Day for recovery." This means that clients are not told that you are back at work until the next day. This allows you to return to the office and catch up without any appointments. Some attorneys automatically take the day off after a large trial, anticipating that they will be exhausted. Some take it even further and schedule a massage, a movie, or some other pleasurable activity the day afterward just to have some relaxing downtime. To maximize your recovery, make it an activity that requires no brainpower.

Use your best judgment about how to take care of yourself during this very stressful period. Take proactive control over the preparation process. Your goal is to avoid having everything occur at the very last minute, leaving you feeling overwhelmed when you walk into the courtroom and unable to mentally assimilate all the information you are dealing with.

Count and Analyze Interruptions

Now that you have taken a more in-depth look at the pervasiveness of interruptions in the law office setting, you are probably anxious to make some changes. The first step toward implementing those changes is to analyze your specific office environment. As the saying goes, "You can't manage what you can't measure," so we have provided you with two tools to assist you in counting and analyzing the characteristics of interruptions you encounter:

- The interruption log
- The interruption analysis worksheet

The Interruption Log

First, keep a record of the number and type of interruptions you encounter on the **Interruption Log** (see Example 7-5). Make a copy of the log and place it on your desk. If you are subject to a great number of interruptions, you may need more than one page per day to capture them all. Keep the log for one or two weeks and note the interruptions that occur daily. You may also want to make copies of the log for your staff. Comparing your information with them may help you find a quicker solution in the analysis phase.

Notice that the form is divided into two parts: the top part is for *external* interruptions and the second part is for *self-imposed* interruptions. Those are the interruptions that *you* create. Note how long the interruption was, what the purpose or the subject was, and whether it involved a person, a phone call, or your environment (e.g., checking e-mail because it beeps every time a new e-mail shows up). Rank the importance of this interruption. Was it an A-level emergency that required you to drop everything? Was it a B-level issue that was not time-sensitive and could have been batched and handled at a planned meeting? Was it a C-level interruption, of very little importance other than socializing? If you use this form for one or two weeks to record the sources of your interruptions, you will be surprised at what you discover.

EXAMPLE 7-5: INTERRUPTION LOG

Briefly describe all interruptions. Include phone calls, attorney/staff/personal crises, drop-in visitors/clients, and visual or audio distractions (i.e., IMs). Keep this log for two weeks. Analyze the results using the evaluation questions provided in Example 7-6, Interruption Log Analysis Worksheet.

External Interruptions

Length of Interruption	Purpose/Subject	Who/What			Importance		
		Person	Phone	Environ	A	B	C

Self-Imposed Interruptions

Length of Interruption	Purpose/Subject	Who/What			Importance		
		Person	Phone	Environ	A	B	C

The Interruption Analysis Worksheet

Once you have kept your Interruption Log for a week or so, you have enough information to begin your analysis by using the **Interruption Analysis Worksheet** in Example 7-6. Make a copy of the worksheet for use in future analyses. The worksheet helps you dissect the information that you collected in your log and determine who or what is habitually interrupting you. If you had your staff participate in the logging of interruptions, you can share information as well. From the analysis, you should begin to see patterns.

- Who or what is responsible for the majority of your interruptions?
- Who or what takes the most time?
- How much time do you spend on interruptions?
- How much time do you want to spend?
- What are some causes and solutions?
- What are you willing to commit to changing?
- What is the big picture regarding interruptions in your firm?

EXAMPLE 7-6: INTERRUPTION LOG ANALYSIS WORKSHEET

1 Review the information you collected on your interruption log. Who are your habitual interrupters? (You may find it helpful to review your findings with other staff members to see if they are experiencing the same types of interruptions.)

_____

_____

_____

2 What else may be occurring in your physical environment that is disruptive: computer alarms, e-mails that beep, texting tones, your ringing and/or vibrating cell phone, loud noises outside your office?

_____

_____

_____

3 Use this chart to help find solutions for underlying causes of your major interruptions as listed in questions 1 and 2. **Write down as many solutions as you can think of, even if they seem impossible or impractical**, such as, "I need my attorney/staff to leave me alone," or, "I need a door!"

_____

_____

_____

4 How many hours per day do you spend handling numbers 1 and 2?

_____

5 How many hours per day should you spend?

_____

6 For the next 30 days, commit to three solutions that are most viable. At the end of 30 days, go back and review your progress. Did you realize a time savings? If so, congratulations! Now, go back to your original log and choose another interrupter to tackle. If one or more of the solutions you chose did not work, reevaluate them using these questions:

◆ What worked and didn't work?

◆ Were the solutions reasonable and realistic?

◆ Are there additional solutions that need to be explored? Should someone else be involved?

◆ How have others in your firm managed? Can you make their solutions work for you?

Rigorously managing your interruptions by setting criteria, identifying the sources of your major time bandits, and committing to their limitation or elimination are the keys to reclaiming concentration time during your workday. You'll discover that your production time does not have to start at five o'clock when the phones stop ringing and everyone else leaves the office.

OTHER TITLES

View all of our books at
www.atticusadvantage.com/books

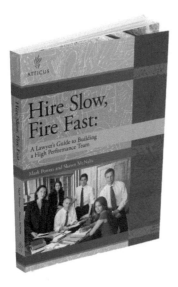

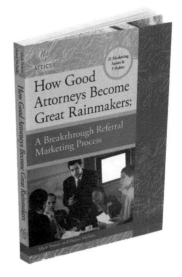

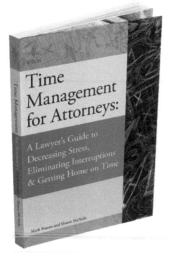

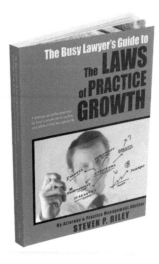

ATTICUS